Shotokan Masters

SHOTOKAN MASTERS

JOSE M. FRAGUAS

EMPIRE Books

P.O. Box 491788, Los Angeles, CA 90049

First published in 2006 by Empire Books.
Copyright © 2006 by Empire Books.

EMPIRE BOOKS
P.O. Box 491788
Los Angeles, CA 90049

First edition
05 04 03 02 01 00 99 98 97 1 3 5 7 9 10 8 6 4 2

Printed in the United States of America.

Library of Congress: 2006009380
ISBN-10: 1-933901-15-2
ISBN-13: 978-1-933901-15-2

Library of Congress Cataloging-in-Publication Data

Fraguas, Jose M.
 Shotokan masters : in their own words / Jose M. Fraguas.
  p. cm.
 Includes index.
 ISBN 1-933901-15-2 (pbk. : alk. paper)
 1. Martial artists. 2. Karate. I. Title.

GV1113.A2F756 2006
796.8092'2--dc22

2006009380

"Before all else, make your mind straight and true."

—Gichin Funakoshi

DEDICATION

I dedicate this book to the memory of Grandmaster Funakoshi Gichin.

Acknowledgments

Many people were responsible for making this book possible, some more directly than others. I want to extend my gratitude to all those whom so generously contributed their time and experience to the preparation of this work. A special thanks to designer Patrick Gross. I also want to thank France's Thierry Plee, long-time friend and president of *Sedirep* and *Budo Editions*; Mr. Schlatt, kind friend and founder of Schlatt-Books in Germany; dear friend, John Cheetham, editor of *Shotokan Karate* magazine in England, your knowledge and support is greatly appreciated; Randall Hassell, author and Karate instructor from St. Louis, Missouri; Nobert Schiffer, President of Satori-Verlag in Germany; Alexander Chichvarin and Oleg Larionov of the Russian National Karate Federation for supplying photos from their personal archives; Don Warrener, director of Rising Sun Productions; Harold E. Sharp, a true legend in the world of martial arts who kindly supplied great photos from his personal archives; Isaac Florentine, film director and passionate karate-ka; Lance Wesbter, editor of the work; and finally to my wife, Julie, whose discernment is always tempered with kindness.

A word of appreciation is also due to my good friend Masahiro Ide, president of *JK Fan* and *Champ* videos, for his generosity and cooperation in this project; I also want to thank the publishers of *Gekkan Karate-do* magazine (Fukushodo, Ltd., Japan), for their assistance, kindness and supply of great photographic material for some of the chapters. Without their support, kindness and commitment to preserve the art of karate-do, this book would not exist.

And last but not least, to all my instructors, past and present, for giving me the understanding and knowledge to undertake all the martial arts projects I've done during my life. My understanding of the art has grown over the years, thanks, in great part, to the questions they made me ask myself. These questions—both perceptive and practical—have sent me further and deeper in search for answers. This book would not exist without you.

You all have my enduring thanks.

—Jose M. Fraguas

CONTENTS

XII
About the Author

XIV
Introduction

1
Tetsuhiko Asai

9
Keinosuke Enoeda

19
Hirokazu Kanazawa

29
Taiji Kase

37
Shojiro Koyama

45
Takayuki Mikami

松濤館

53

Masatoshi Nakayama

61

Hidetaka Nishiyama

71

Tsutomu Ohshima

81

Teruyuki Okazaki

87

Yoshiharu Osaka

93

Osamu Ozawa

99

Masahiko Tanaka

105

Mikio Yahara

111

Koss Yokota

ABOUT THE AUTHOR

Born and raised in Madrid, Spain, Jose M. Fraguas began his martial arts studies with judo, in grade school, at age 9. From there he moved to taekwon-do and then to kenpo-karate, earning black belts in both styles. During this same period, he also studied shito-ryu karate under Japanese Masters Masahiro Okada and Yashunari Ishimi, eventually receiving a fifth-degree black belt and the title of *Shihan* from Soke Mabuni Kenzo. He began his career as a writer at age 16 as a regular contributor to martial arts magazines in Great Britain, France, Spain, Italy, Germany, Portugal, Holland and Australia.

In 1980, he moved to Los Angeles, California, where his open-minded mentality helped him to develop a realistic approach to the martial arts. Seeking to supplement his previous training, he researched other disciplines such as jiu-jitsu, escrima and muay Thai.

In 1986, Fraguas founded his own publishing company in Europe, authoring dozens of books and distributing his magazines to 35 countries in three different languages. His reputation and credibility as a martial artist and publisher became well known to the top masters around the world. Considering himself a martial artist first and a writer and publisher second, Fraguas feels fortunate to have had the opportunity to interview many legendary martial artists. He recognizes that much of the information given in the interviews helped him to discover new dimensions in the martial arts. "I was constantly absorbing knowledge from the great masters," he recalls. "I only trained with a few of them, but intellectually and spiritually all of them have made very important contributions to my growth as a complete martial artist."

Steeped in tradition yet looking to the future, Fraguas understands and appreciates martial arts history and philosophy and feels this rich heritage is a necessary steppingstone to personal growth and spiritual evolution. His desire to promote both ancient philosophy and modern thinking provided the motivation for writing this book. "If the motivation is just money, a book cannot be of good quality," Fraguas says. "If the book is written to just make people happy, it cannot be deep. I want to write books so I can learn as well as teach. Karate-do, like human life itself, is filled with experiences that seem quite ordinary at the time and assume a fabled stature only with the passage of the years. I hope this work will be appreciated by future practitioners of the art of Shotokan karate."

Originally from Madrid, Spain, he is currently living in Los Angeles, California. ◉

INTRODUCTION

Some of my best days were spent interviewing and meeting the masters appearing in this book. Having long conversations with them allowed me to do more than simply scratch the surface of the technical aspects of the shotokan style of karate, but to also research and analyze the human beings behind the teachers. Some of the dialogues began by simply commenting about the superficial techniques of fighting, and ended up turning into a very uncommon spiritual conversation about the philosophical aspects of the martial arts. I have been honored and fortunate of having the opportunity of training under some of them and unfortunate for not have trained under the rest of them. All of them have been important in my formation as martial artist and karate-ka. And to all of them, I owe deeply.

Interestingly enough, none of the men behind the masters were interested in trying to prove their style was the best—it was just the opposite. The essence of their whole message was very far from that. These teachers are most interested in fostering, through their teachings, the development of good human beings. They are trying to pass along a culture, a discipline, and an education to the generations to follow. Being better than someone or something else is simply something they don't care about. Although they are all very different, they all share a common thread of the traditional values such as discipline, respect, positive attitude, dedication, and etiquette.

Their different origins and backgrounds heavily influenced them but never prevented them from analyzing, researching, or modifying anything that they considered appropriate. They always kept an open mind to improving both their arts and themselves and took the teachings of the original shotokan art to a higher level of expression. From a formal philosophical point of view many of them follow the wisdom of Zen and Taoism—others just use common sense.

Years before anyone ever heard of any of them, they devoted themselves to their arts, often in solitude, sometimes to the exclusion of other pursuits most of us take for granted. They worked themselves into extraordinary physical condition and stayed there. They ignored distractions and diversions and brought to their training a great deal of concentration. The best of them got as good as they could possibly get at performing and teaching their chosen art, and the rest of us watched them and, leading our balanced lives, wondered how good we might have gotten at something had we devoted ourselves to whatever we did as ferociously as these masters embraced their arts. In that respect they bear our dreams.

They focus their teachings on how to use the martial arts to become a better person. Of course, the functionality of their systems was and is something they care about, but it is not the focal point of their lives or their training. Eastern and Western mentally is very different—like night and day. Fortunately, there are many links that, once discovered, open a wide spectrum of possibilities not only to martial arts but to a better existence as human beings.

"The masters are gone," many like to say, but as long as we keep their teachings in our hearts, they will live forever. To understand the art of karate properly it is necessary to take into account the philosophical and psychological methods as well as the physical techniques. There is a deep distinction between a fighting system and a martial art, and a general feeling in the martial arts community is that the roots of the martial arts have been de-emphasized, neglected, or totally abandoned. Martial arts are not a sport—they are very different. Someone who chooses to devote themselves to a sport such as basketball, tennis, soccer, or football, which is based on youth, strength, and speed chooses to die twice. When you can no longer do a certain sport, due to the lack of any one of those attributes, waking up in the morning without the activity and purpose that has been the center of your day for 25 years is spooky. Martial arts can and should be practiced for life. They are not sports, they are a "way of life."

To find out what karate-do means to you, what it does for you, and what it holds for you, is a deeply personal process. Each path is different and we all have to find a personal rhythm that fit us individually, according to what surround us.

As human beings, we are always tempted to follow linear logic towards ultimate self-improvement—but the truth is that there are no absolute truths. You have to find your own way in life whether it be in martial arts, business or cherry picking. Whatever path you pursue, you have to distill the personal truths that are right for you, according to your own nature. The quest for perfection is very imperfect, and not in tune with human nature or experience. To have any hope of attaining even a single perfection, you have to concentrate on a single pursuit and direct all your energy towards it. In this sense, perfection comes from appreciating endeavors for their own sake—not to impress anyone—but for your own inner satisfaction and sense of accomplishment.

It is important to have a feeling of responsibility; and putting yourself into an art as genuinely as you can, without any sense that you are going to get something back in return, reverberates throughout time and space. We need to honor those who came before us, as well as nurture those who will come after, so the art can grow and expand—you've got to send the elevator back down.

Martial arts are a large part of my life and I draw inspiration from them. I really don't know the "how" or the "why" of their effect on me, but I feel their influence in even my most mundane activities. All human beings have sources or principles that keep them grounded, and martial arts are mine. That is when the term "way of life" becomes real. In bushido, the self-discipline required to pursue mastery is more important than mastery itself—the struggle is more important than the reward. A common thread throughout the lives of all the masters is their constant struggle towards self-mastery. They realized that life is an ongoing process, and once you achieve all your goals you are as good as dead. But this process is not all driven by action. Often the greatest action is inaction, and the hardest voice to hear is the sound of your own thoughts. You need to sit alone and collect yourself, free from technology and distraction, and just think. This is perhaps the only way to achieve mental and spiritual clarity.

It would be wonderful to find a single martial artist who combined all the great qualities of these masters—but that's impossible. That, however, was one of the things that inspired me to write this book. I wanted to preserve some things that they said a long time ago, that not many people today are aware of. These are true shotokan masters…in their own words.

Tetsuhiko
ASAI

I was born in Shikoku in 1935. I studied judo and kendo before getting involved in karate at Takushoku University. This is where Grandmaster Funakoshi, Nakayama Sensei and Okazaki Sensei were in charge of the training. I entered the JKA instructor's course. After I graduated, I was sent to Hawaii and Taiwan to teach the art. It was in Taiwan where I had the opportunity to meet several Chinese kung-fu masters with whom I shared training and knowledge. Some people approached me to learn and others challenged me, so I had to fight. I still keep in touch with some of my friends from my time in China.

My father was a very strong man and many people considered him an eccentric. He was very strict with me, and he had an ironclad code of ethics. He always said that once you begin something you can't stop. You must finish it. I respect my father very highly and this sense of commitment has been the guiding principle of my life.

TRAINING

Hard training is important. You have to put your mind into it. Strive to find a good instructor; learn the right technique, timing, kime and the proper use of the body; and use your natural energy.

You should strive to control every part of your body at will. This is a true sign of mastery, and it goes beyond any style. The important thing is to perform the technique with a certain spirit in a certain atmosphere. This is one of the main principles we were trying to develop at the old JKA. We wanted to use the human body in the most efficient way for the martial arts. Once you follow this rule, you'll see an infinite amount of possibilities, although the human body is limited. In fact, the only limit in martial arts training is the limit of the human body.

In order to practice karate properly, you need to learn how to relax the muscles and use them properly to generate speed. If your muscles are not relaxed, they simply can't be fast and you can't produce power. It is necessary to know how to relax the muscles and use the natural energy of your body. Karate is good for health, so students need to find out how to do it right. Unfortunately, many instructors around the world never learnt the right way and always practiced with tension and hard movements. This is one of the reasons why people think karate is a hard style while the truth is that it is not. It is important to look at the art from a softer point of view.

Flexibility is an open door for relaxation, and I make this principle

my main objective. It is important to try to keep all joints loose and supple. I have tried everything, and I am constantly learning and absorbing. I am not an expert in every style I practice, but I have picked up the ones I could do well and that suited my personal style.

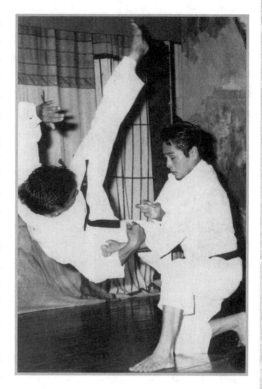

The martial arts have been around for a long time, and the ancestors based their styles on natural movement and relaxation. Today, people don't want to use the old traditional methods to use both physical and inner strength because it is easier to lift weights. There is no reason why the old and new methods can't work together, but it is important to understand how both work and the direction you want to take in your training. Weightlifting creates muscle mass and a rapid increase in strength, but this kind of training works against the relaxation necessary for karateka to generate

TEACHING

My teaching is for health, and that's the reason why I emphasize relaxation all the time. Making the muscles tense is not good for your body and can cause many injuries during training. I want the students to learn and understand how to use the body properly and how to produce the right kime without using useless movements or unnecessary tension.

Karate has five different aspects that should be developed. First, there is the martial side of it or the combative and self-preservation of the individual. Second, the health benefits derived from its practice. Third, is the physical activity, which is always good. Fourth, the sportive element that brings people together. Last but not least is the development of character and spirit. My approach to teaching includes all of these elements because I consider them all necessary.

SELF-DEFENSE

Self-defense is a whole different situation. Attack the eyes, the throat, the groin, the knee and all the vital areas where you can infringe a lot of pain with simple natural weapons. If you train with this concept in mind, you'll always have real karate in your hands. You will also have an effective karate, and this will bring self-confidence to you.

It is not about muscle; it is about knowing what tool to use and what targets to hit. The art of karate is practiced barehanded and its essence is to render an opponent unable to fight by using a single technique. If you want to put a nail all the way into a piece of wood, you don't use a screwdriver. You use a hammer. Learn what weapons are more appropriate to hit certain parts of the human body, especially when you have to protect yourself against a much bigger aggressor.

JKA KARATE

The late Grandmaster Funakoshi established the roots, Nakayama Sensei developed the foundation and now it is up to us to expand the art in different ways to meet the current needs of students and society. Many people may think that my style of teaching is very strange, but this is only because I emphasize aspects that we usually don't see in regular karate. I am now researching ways of training for life. I'm trying to develop techniques and training methods that we can use until we die. It's an unlimited world, and we must try to expand. It is like a telescope. Don't look down the wrong end at a little circle; look through the wide end so you can see more.

True karate is capable of adapting to the situation and changing accordingly. That is the essence of life. Change is simply the product of education. The more you learn, the more you realize other things. The Chinese seem to be more natural and casual when doing things, and that affects the way they train and conceive the martial arts. In karate, we have the same movements and principles, but you have to look closely to discover them.

All of the head instructors of the old JKA trained and practiced the same kata. However, when one [of them] left Japan and lived for 30 years in another country, it was logical that some changes (his feelings and teaching methods) were going to occur. This is natural, and there is nothing wrong with that. The essence of the form is still there and nothing has changed, but the personal flavor the instructor put into it [changed] because of his evolution as a martial artist.

SPORT

Karate is a martial art—not a sport. The sport aspect of karate has allowed the art to spread greatly. In itself, that is not particularly bad, but it sure brings consequences if you do not watch out. Competition has changed a lot throughout the years. In the old days, it was more of a one-punch, one-kill [mentality]. We really were aware of any possibility and making a single mistake meant defeat. That is the true spirit of Budo, and this spirit can be maintained in modern competition. That's why I like the idea of shobu-ippon. It represents what true Budo is. Sport karate is only a very small part of karate. I have great students who are tournament champions, but this doesn't prevent them from training real Budo karate. In competition karate, you can always find shortcuts to win. In traditional karate, there are no shortcuts of any kind. It is important that the public has a clear idea of what is and is not the art of karate

KATA

Kata represents the history of the art. All the tradition in these forms has been passed down from masters to students throughout the

generations. The kata were structured and formatted by the old masters to preserve realistic knowledge of self-defense. It is very important to study the form and to understand what you are doing and why are you doing it. It's occasionally difficult to completely decipher the bunkai and realistic applications of kata movements because they are not so obvious at first. The main idea is to use the kata as a training method and the bunkai as the actual application in combat. It is very important to link the actual form with the application against an opponent. You can also use different kata to develop different attributes and qualities. Not all kata are designed for the same thing.

BUDO

With the creation of Japan Karate Shotokai, I simply wanted to express karate in my own way. Karate has taught me to overcome my fears and myself and to get along with and work with others. I am an engineer of the art … not a politician. I want to train and teach people … not argue about things. I don't have time for that. I want to create collaboration and support among the students.

Life is very short, and I have a lot of things I want to do and accomplish. I'm a martial artist, not a politician. I always welcome anyone who wants to train with me, regardless of his association with other karate groups. I like to do karate and not waste time talking and arguing.

To truly understand what Budo means, you have to put your heart into it and never stop training. Budo is Japanese culture, and sometimes it is hard for non-Japanese to understand. That's why it is important that students first understand their own culture and then absorb what Budo can offer.

Karate—like a human being—needs time to grow. There is no end to expanding. Consider yourself always a student and never think that you are already there. Never give up. ◉

Keinosuke
Enoeda

I was born in Fukuoka on the island of Kyushu in southern Japan on July 4, 1935, and practiced martial arts from an early age. While my brother and sister played games, at the age of 7 I began judo. I continued my training through high school, where I regularly entered judo competitions and was runner-up in the All-Japan High School Championships. At the age of 17, shortly after I gained my second degree black belt, I watched a demonstration given by two members of the Takushoku University Karate Club in Tokyo. I was won over. Aside from any academic merits, Takushoku University was well known for its strong martial arts, particularly its tough karate team, and this was my main reason for enrolling at the university.

After two years training I passed my *sho-dan* examination, and then two years later, at age 21, I was made captain of the karate club. It was during my university training that I received instruction from the great master, Funakoshi Gichin. Master Funakoshi was very old when I met him, but one thing that I still recall is that once he put the gi on, his whole attitude and body movement changed immediately. It was like he received some kind of external energy by wearing the karate gi. The transformation in his physical movements was amazing.

9

After graduating in 1957 with a degree in Commerce, I was invited to take the special instructors course at JKA headquarters. I accepted and for the next three years studied long and hard on a daily basis under Masatoshi Nakayama, the chief instructor of the JKA, and Hidetaka Nishiyama, a leading senior. I regularly entered various tournaments and achieved several victories, including the East University Karate Championships. Then in 1961 I won third place in the *kumite* division of the JKA All-Japan Championships and also finished high in the *kata* event. The following year I repeated my kata placing and moved another step up in the kumite by finishing second—losing to Hiroshi Shirai. Then in 1963, after another year's hard preparation, I turned the tables on Shirai in the kumite finals and became the All-Japan Champion, and again placed as a kata finalist.

In the beginning, karate-do was an art practiced by a select few under the founder of a particular style. In those days, the art had a great deal of morality and dignity. A good karate-do student would never show off—and even in combat was expected to not use the art unless completely necessary. Of course, things have changed today but the essence and heart of the art should still be the same.

Up until my 1963 triumph, I had only taught locally at the Tokyo Art College and a military university. Among the spectators at that year's championships was President Sukarno of Indonesia and he negotiated for my services. Together with Master Nakayama, I spent four months in Indonesia teaching the his personal bodyguards and also at various police and military establishments. Following the JKA's policy of sending its best instructors out from Japan to spread shotokan karate, I began my worldwide travels that were to culminate in my settling in Great Britain as the shotokan chief instructor.

KATA & BUNKAI

The importance attached to kata makes it one of the most recognizable features in all of martial arts. Kata was the creation of the most important teachers of each style of karate in the past. They formalized their knowledge and made a set of practical techniques to pass to their students. They systematized this huge amount of knowledge in forms that have been preserved throughout the years. They recorded for posterity the physical movements they came as a result of them risking their lives in actual contests.

When studying kata, we can see a model for a particular method of certain techniques. There is a formalized way of doing things but kata also offers freedom of expression. Not only the techniques of the creator, but also the acquisition of the right state of mind called *kokoro*. Kata must be memorized, incorporated into one's own being and then mastered to perfection. It is essential to break into areas of techniques that are original. Kata training offers a way of understand other aspects of human existence, that's why is so important not to study the form from a strictly structural point of view. All traditional katas are greatly respected in the martial arts, and you can search your entire life to find the deeper meanings of a particular form.

Moreover, the beauty of refinement (*kohga*) and the elegant simplicity (*sabi*) are also important kata training elements.

If we simply focus on training the external movements (*waza*), without also analyzing the state of mind behind the form, it will be impossible to practice the true art of karate-do. Kata has dignity in its severity and is extreme in its beauty. Simply said, kata is physical movements by each individual. Due to this fact, it is possible to continue to train for the acquisition of technique and mind even when we are old. People tend to be really attracted to sparring, but a true karate-ka must stop and look very careful about the role kata plays in the art.

When doing kata you must live the form. Each kata must be done full-out. If done correctly, the karate-ka will reach his physical limits and not be able to continue. He'll be near his end. You shouldn't endlessly repeat a kata. To do so is to show that one is not living the kata. Only on certain occasion will one repeat a kata a number of times—and that is for mental and spiritual purposes—to force you to go beyond the body, the mind and the art. You have to live the kata. Use all your power as if in life or death. This is something that sport karate does not have. This is why kata is important. The body is trained, the mind is trained, and the understanding of the technique deepens.

It is in kata , where we can find the answer. The kata keeps the

meaning of the technique deep. It makes one fresh to respond. Knowledge of the art increases because self-defense is found in kata. Without kata training, the body cannot properly understand the technique There will be no calm and no confidence. With kata training, one is capable at all times—and calm and confident of their ability. With the self-assurance gained from kata, there is little need to ever use karate for self-defense.

Bunkai is the practical application of the kata. It is very important that the student understands the application of the technique. Many times students do not understand kata because they cannot see the meaning of the movement they are doing. They see slow, broad movements and tend to think that kata has no purpose. Bunkai shows them the purpose. As the student advances in his study, his understanding of the tech-

niques becomes deeper and more profound. Each technique improves his precision and kime. Kata helps karate-ka to understand the many uses the techniques and how to apply them.

SPORT

Sport karate is a definite aspect of karate-do. Competition is not bad. It is good for the spirit. It is specifically good for the spirit when the proper etiquette—win or lose—is present. Sport karate is also a demanding test of one's individual ability. It is also a good test of the mind and one's control of power. And if etiquette and sportsmanship is present, it is always good for the spirit. To many people today tend to train simply for competition. Sport sparring is not self-defense and has very little to do with it. Sparring is a test of ability, but ability of a different kind. Winning competitions is not the true meaning karate—it is not enough just to do the techniques correctly. Those whose execute the techniques without true heart cannot call themselves true karate-ka. Karate-do is many things at once. It is budo. It is being fit and calm. It develops good character and confidence. It is crisp and powerful physical movements. It can be a sport and at the same time be a complete self-defense method. Karate competition has become increasingly popular, and gradually the true heart of karate has almost been forgotten. Modern karate-ka must think about the true root of the art and try to understand the essence of it deeply.

Without this deep understanding, it will be difficult for future generations to know what the real art is about.

TRAINING

If you train hard and consistently, one day you are going to come face-to-face with what is called a "brick wall." This stage is also known as "hitting the wall," or reaching a "plateau." In order to progress and follow real karate-do, you must be able to break through the wall—one step at a time and brick by brick. Only by destroying this obstacle will you succeed. Only then can you reach a higher level of technical mastery. Unfortunately, many reach this wall and do not succeed in breaking through. Thus, they limit themselves. This not only happens in martial arts, but in many other aspects of life. After you have succeeded in conquering your 'brick wall' in any field, you will have a feeling of true achievement. This is because you met a challenge and broke out of a difficult period. This will build confidence and bring about great results. This is when karate-do becomes a practical way of life and not a mere physical exercise.

Technique, because of the tournament training, can become weak. The practitioner's techniques can becomes shallow because certain moves work best in sport karate. This means that one can devote all his time to practicing these techniques. This works against the true spirit of karate and all martial arts. There are many techniques in karate-do. In budo karate-do, not sport karate, one must know and develop all these techniques—not just two or three. The way to avoid this is intensive kata training. This is how I trained in my youth in Japan. Before competition we would train kata, kata and more kata. Only at the end of the session would there be one-step sparring. Don't focus excessively on sparring before a tournament; train kata. Then immediately before the tournament, move to one-step kumite, and then just few days before the tournament day, concentrate on free-sparring. You'll be amazed by the results—especially when you win the kata division the same day!

KUMITE

Taking part in a match is a big responsibility as well as a great opportunity for both yourself as an individual and the organization to which you belong. In your journey through life, it is important to study and learn how to seize an opportunity and gain victory by displaying your own powerful ability. Composure, courage, sharpness, precision and courtesy must all be present in your waza when you move your entire body—not merely your hands and feet. In an instant every part of you moves in unison.

In order to win the match it is of great value to know your opponent and to know yourself. If your opponent is unknown to you, you should get to know him before your fight—paying attention to his strong points and favorite techniques. Then, after accumulating vast experience in the course of many matches, you will become very

sharp in your observations and be able to recognize your opponent's strong and weak points at first sight.

When the time comes to fight, you must not think in terms of simply winning, but you should feel delighted that you have attained your long-cherished chance to compete. This will help you to focus and to defeat fear. When you have vanquished your own fear, then you will be ready to fight against your opponent—whoever he may be.

When you stand face-to-

15

face with your opponent, the first thing you want is to make him feel that your energy will overwhelm him. The second thing is not to miss any of his movement—even slight ones—and at the same time act as if you were engulfing the opponent's whole body with the inside of your hands and feet. Even if your opponent is a strong and experienced practitioner you must not fear him. By the same token, if your opponent is weak and inexperienced you must not underestimate him. Always fight every match with your maximum power.

When you attack, do not forget to protect yourself with defensive maneuvers, but just remember that defense alone won't win the fight. Attack with right posture, correct spirit and precise techniques. Strive to be the one who always takes the initiative. If you act before your opponent moves, you will go on to victory. This is, I think, the most important point of all.

Good karate-ka should have good control, so there is no need for excessive contact. If there is too much contact, then there is a chance of injury if the technique is delivered with power. It is necessary to develop good control so that you can control the amount of body contact when you reach the target. The problem appears when the competing karate-ka doesn't have control due to insufficient training

at the dojo. Then as a referee, you have to deal with the problem in the competition. What the teachers should do is train students correctly and don't allow them to compete until they have the proper skill to control their punches and kicks.

BUDO

True budo is many things. Sport karate is OK, but you must practice kata as well. Kata training is very necessary for taking part in sport karate. This keeps techniques fresh and it is also important because it develops the body properly. It is necessary to keep fit for the art. Kata teaches how each technique is to be performed in terms of body movements. It conditions the body and the mind. With kata training you reach a higher level of fitness. All you techniques are sharp and fresh. You have been drilling and exercising the body, extending your knowledge of tactics, techniques, and applications. This keeps one fresh and also insures that all the techniques will have the right amount of power and precision.

In every karate match, victory is of prime importance; however, since a karate match is based on budo, you cannot use any means to defeat your opponent. In a karate match you must fight strictly under the true spirit of budo and play fair in order to be victorious. This is the right way to win.

I come from a very traditional background and karate is part of my nature. It affects the way I look at things and how I lead my life. Karate taught me discipline, and with discipline a person can continue karate practice for many years. My objective was and still is, to train everyday regardless of the weather or the condition I'm in. I never neglect my daily training. I haven't missed a day's training since a very young age. I believe my everyday effort, plus my judo and kendo practice when I was very young, helped to develop my mental and physical strength. This strength as a human being has helped me to achieve my goals throughout my life.

All practitioners should remember to train in true budo karate-do. Do sport karate if you like, but always focus your mind and body on the perfection of yourself as a human being. This is true karate-do. And no matter where your interests lead you, remember that kata is the vehicle that will allow you to reach a true understanding of real karate. ◉

Hirokazu
Kanazawa

When I started karate training, the first year included a lot of running. The dojo at Takushoku University was so small that the losers of the race were eliminated from karate class. This built spirit. You must never forget that your the purpose of training is to master the art of karate, and to do so one has to develop perseverance, patience, and imagination to survive the ups and downs of being in the dojo.

TAI CHI

I began my tai chi training when I went to Hawaii to teach for the JKA. Later on, I met Mr. Yang, who is a member of the family tree of the Yang family style of tai chi when he came to the JKA to learn karate. I had the feeling that he was already practicing another martial art but he didn't say anything. I began training under him around 1957 and I haven't stopped since.I don't practice tai chi for tai chi, but for my karate. After I started training in tai chi, I began to really understand how to keep and develop a healthy body, mind, and spirit. In the beginning, tai chi was very difficult, I couldn't use any tension at all and had to force myself to relax all my muscles. You see, I was trying to do tai chi with karate power, and it was painful trying

19

to move with no force at all. My body felt really uncomfortable but after a couple of years of training I began to understand and developed a natural softness that still retained the real strength in the technique.

During my first year of training I was very frustrated with tai chi and even my stomach used to make weird noises. Mr. Yang told me once that the reason was that I had no internal power and my body was protesting! The human body changes and your martial art has to change with it. And this has to be done using internal power because it strengthens the internal organs. There is a point in every karate practitioner's life where the punch's unifying force must no longer be rooted in the muscles but in the internal organs.

I don't think that is a good idea try to combine karate and tai chi. I feel it is better to study them separately. But even although they are opposites, the study of both brings a more balanced view. Tai chi has allowed me to step outside of karate in much the same way as you need to step outside your house to fully appreciate it. From the inside, you do not have a complete view of it. This act of stepping outside afforded me a chance to see karate from an entirely different point of view and to appreciate it even more.

AGE

I am much older and I will honestly tell you that my body is not as supple as it used to be and does not respond as quickly as it once did. This is a physiological reality and is perfectly normal—that's why I adapted my karate to the needs of my body and why tai chi has been of a great benefit to me. I have many students who did not start karate until they were fifty years old and they all get do quite well.

KOBUDO

Kobudo was never practiced in the JKA, but it is interesting that there is some evidence of Master Funakoshi Gichin using the sai for training.

I started my kobudo training in Okinawa, and when I returned to Japan I tried it for myself. At that time I knew the basics only. My teacher told me that there was no kobudo kata. So I devised some kata myself. Many people twirl the nunchaku, but this doesn't allow real power to develop. In kata training one learns concentration and how to develop smoothness in motion in order to create devastating striking power. I train in bo, sai and nunchaku. When you're using the nunchaku, your arms must be relaxed and soft—"empty" is the right word—no tense muscles. In nunchaku training if you move the weapon with tension, then you lose power. The same is true in tai chi.

Kobudo training may not be important for everyone, but it is for me. I truly consider karate and kobudo part of the same family. Therefore, if I learn kobudo I will better understand the history of karate.

SPORT

I believe it is quite a confusing period for karate students. They really don't know if they are practicing a sport or a martial art. Sport is an aspect of karate but it is not everything. Unfortunately, karate today is neither a sport nor a martial art, and that's very confusing for the students. I think it would be better if sport karate evolved separately from the martial art side.

Sport is good as long as it is regarded as a recreation that you can leave and then go back to karate budo. Competition by itself is bad for the art, because you will understand nothing. Sport is open and enjoyable. Karate is not always enjoyable, because it is never easy to do the right thing. Karate is for the self. In sport we win over an opponent—in karate, we win over the self. In budo, a good kata performer must be a good fighter and vice versa. To realize the spirit of budo, one must be good at both kata and kumite—both sides have to be taught. The positive and the negative balance is very important. Good things always come in twos. In sport karate, one is only good at kata or kumite.

Tournaments are OK, but the practitioner has to understand more than only sport. Usually the practitioner is disappointed when the point goes against him because winning is everything, and he understands nothing else. A person like this is very dangerous to society because he respects only himself. If you respect your opponent, you'll never start a war. Everything connects to karate. True budo is good for society.

JKA & SKIF

I never wanted to create my own organization and that was never my goal. When I was in Europe, making plans to go to Montreal University in Canada to teach for a few months, I sent a letter of resignation to the JKA—not as a JKA instructor—but as the director of a section of the JKA. I just didn't feel I could function in that capacity while I was out of the country. Three months later, when I returned to Europe, I received a letter from the JKA informing me

that I was summarily dismissed. I was completely shocked. Giving up would have been against the budo spirit of everything I had been taught. So I decided that if the JKA was against me, I had to defend myself.

In the beginning, many people said that SKIF would only last a couple of months. Fortunately, as you can see, we are still going strong. I want to emphasize that I never wanted to leave the JKA. Some people said that I deserted

Nakayama Sensei, but the truth is that I never wanted to be independent because that's not in my spirit. But I had to defend myself. A samurai must not be frightened—even of death.

PURE KARATE

Pure shotokan does not exist. The JKA practices a type of shotokan—but it is the shotokan of the JKA. Ohshima Sensei practices a shotokan but again it is his shotokan. Each master has a different view, a different brain, a different comprehension of things.

I have been fortunate of study different karate styles under other great teachers. I sometimes invite instructors of different styles to teach at my dojo and also I visit other dojo and occasionally teach. I researched shorin-ryu, uechi-ryu, goju-ryu, and others, because I really believe that no karate style is complete. We must look to the different roots. That's why I decided train in Okinawan styles. After all, they are the root of karate. Unfortunately, some organizations forbid this. This close-minded thinking is driven by politics, not karate.

MAKIWARA

As a young student, I used to punch the makiwara more than 1,000 times daily, which is not correct. This kind of training is very important for karate but only with 50 or 60 full-powered blows per hand. It's important to develop power, speed and kime. I remember my knuckles were split open to the bone during my early training sessions. Once I went to see a doctor who cleaned the wounds and wrapped my hands! My sen-pai almost kicked me out of the dojo!

MY KARATE

I didn't modify the karate I was taught but I did try to go back to its roots. Not to kung fu but to kong fu. Kong fu was a healthy exercise for mind and body. Daruma developed Zen exercises for internal power. This is very hard training and the students should never stop or they will never understand. In history, there was always a trend to improve health exercises for self-defense techniques. I haven't changed karate, I just kept it within the historical tradition.

The karate that I teach is a product of more than thirty years of spiritual and physical research into the true meaning of martial arts. Perhaps because of my training in tai chi and kobudo, some karateka look at me differently. Also, it may be due to my very personal perception of karate—I teach for everybody, not only for the young and the strong. For me, karate is unlimited and is a form of self-administered therapeutic massage. It is not just a sport. For instance, my tsuki has developed considerably since my younger days—but it happened subconsciously. I now have a double kime—a physical focus first, and then a speed focus, which delivers more shock. I did not realize what I was doing until it was pointed out to me by Matsuda Ryuchi, a very famous authority on Chinese martial arts. He mentioned that my punch was from Chinese kempo—but I was unaware of that. The same happened in other aspects.

Performing karate like a machine, without the proper relaxation, correct posture and breathing, will cause problems. That's the reason why I make my karate "self-chiropractic." Karate should improve health, not cause injuries.

KATA

Some people think that I have changed kata, but I never did. After five years of kata training, two people can practice the same movement and look identical—but after ten years differences emerge. They may think that they are doing the same movement, but since the body, character, and thoughts are different it is only natural that the kata will be different. Kata must look good for the referees, but at the same time must not be changed for aesthetics to create an extra flourish.

IMPORTANT POINTS

Breathing, movement and timing are the most important aspects of true karate—but breathing is first. The very first thing we do in this world is to breathe—but 90 percent of the population do not know how to breath correctly. If your breathing is wrong, your body will be wrong and your mind will be wrong also. There is a very strong connection. You control your spirit with your breathing and should always be thinking and trying to learn more about this most vital aspect, since it is the very core of life. I always stress the philosophical and health aspects of karate and try to explain the reason behind the techniques.

For instance, when I'm teaching the tsuki I do not show a punch to hit someone, I relate the movement to the person's hara—his center. I explain in the tsuki, that you should always push the head straight because it will promote good health by sending blood and oxygen into the head, which nourishes the cells. Utilizing the correct breathing, the hara, the concentration, and the impact produces a slight vibration on the vertebral column, which communicates to the brain and produces a sort of massaging effect. Remember that basic movements must be good for health; if not, then they are not good for human life.

In the beginning I did not teach so much about breathing, but I adhered to a power style—quite a natural thing when I was young because at that age you favor strength. But with time and thought, I have come to a realization that winning can be done using only 60 percent of your power—100 percent is not necessary if you have good technique. If I use 60 percent correctly and then use 40 percent

of my opponent's power against him, the total is still 100 percent and the combination will result in more damage to him. This approach is the result of my tai chi studies.

YESTERDAY AND TODAY

Two hundred years ago, bushi was OK. It was a matter of being strong without caring about health or anything else because there was a continuous life and death struggle. One had to be strong and have no fear in order to face daily life. Now, things have changed in society, and it is more important to be healthy in body and mind. Our character must be more peaceful but still having the same bushido spirit.

If I could train as I like, I'd be in even better condition, but sometimes is impossible due to meetings, visitors, business, et cetera. I believe a good karate-ka must use his body and his mind, so I study and read also. This gives a practitioner a much stronger quality—a balanced personality. It is important to understand that the body changes and one loses the power of the muscles as you age. You cannot retain physical power forever. At some point you must develop the power of the internal organs. When you're older, the power of the spirit is what shapes your karate.

KUMITE

Kumite is very important to "harmonize oneself with the opponent." I know this is a very difficult concept to understand until the practitioner is able to experience by himself. The basic idea is to establish harmony within yourself—harmonize your breathing, your movements, and your power. This will lead you to harmonize with the opponent and with this kind of harmony your opponent will be unable to find a good moment to attack you and it will be very difficult for him to beat you. Only then will you be able to use and combine sen no sen, and go no sen. You must work in harmony with your opponent and not against him.

There are schools where the students start free-sparring almost immediately. With this way it might be possible to improve quickly, but you will never reach the higher levels. The bottom line is that if you don't train extensively in the basics, you cannot reach the higher stages of martial arts. The kihon are just the basic techniques, but a thorough grounding in those will teach your body to instantly understand what is required in combat. The idea is to merge the body and mind. You should be able to perform any movement without thinking. This is the real meaning and purpose of the kihon.

FUTURE

I would like to see all karate-ka work to understand the real spirit of karate—the breathing control and the cultivation of hara. My philosophy is to always be true to myself and to others. I can honestly say that I fear nothing, not even death—and I do not mean this in a big-headed or conceited way. I simply always try my best in everything I do, so I will be satisfied when I die. I think the reason that people fear death is because they want to accomplish so many things that are left undone—they feel their life is unfinished. In karate, there is no secret other than hard training. This is the real spirit of karate. ☻

Taiji

Kase

When I was 6 I began training in judo since my father was a judo teacher. Judo was much better known during the war, but I started practicing karate in 1944 at the shotokan dojo, where Master Funakoshi was imparting his knowledge of the art of the empty hand. I remember one day I was in a bookstore and I saw a book written by Master Funakoshi. Of course, I knew about judo, aikido and kendo, but karate was something new to me. I decided then to go to his dojo. This dojo was destroyed by the American Air Force in 1945. This is a very important memory to me because many other great karate instructors never had the chance to train and learn from Master Funakoshi at his original dojo. I'll keep that memory until the last day in my life and beyond. Sensei Egami and Sensei Hironishi were also my teachers. They helped Funakoshi Yoshitaka in assisting Funakoshi Gichin. I remember that around 1946 Sensei Hironishi was helping Gichen Funakoshi. I also trained under Yoshitaka, his son.

Master Tsuomu Ohshima, who now resides in California, was also training there with me. Ohshima was only 13 years old when I was the university captain already. My university was Senshin, and Sensei Ohshima went to Komazawa. I used to collect Sensei

Funakoshi to go to training. Both the atmosphere and the spirit at the old dojo was very special—very different from the other schools. I firmly believe that there was some kind of magic there. The training we did then with sword was perfectly applicable to the empty-hand methods of karate. We were living in a time of war so the martial spirit was everywhere. We didn't think about tournaments or sport. It was touch and kill, very much like katana training. This was the true age of budo!

Yoshitaka Funakoshi Sensei was really fast and strong. His movements were truly powerful—like a tiger. He was good at everything. Unfortunately, at 38 he was already very sick. Sometimes he had to stop in the middle of the training and go to a corner to rest. Then he would apologize and return to train—even harder. He had been told at 12 years old that his illness had no cure. I guess he wanted to reach a higher spiritual level by training without limits. I truly believe this was the reason for his extraordinary ability and skill in the art.

GICHIN FUNAKOSHI

Sensei Funakoshi was continually changing and improving the art. I would say that he liberated karate from the precepts of Okinawan karate. On the other hand, he was a very honest and calm man—very kind and with a deep spirituality. Sensei Funakoshi was constantly changing and making innovations to the art. He was from Okinawa and when he moved to Japan he saw how other martial arts systems like judo had great recognition from the government and the people. He wished the same thing for karate-do. He wanted karate-do to be part of the budo arts. For Master Funakoshi, karate was not a sport but a way of life. He always advised us to practice and keep practicing all the time. In fact, the training we did then with swords was perfectly applicable to karate! Don't forget we were living in a time of war and there was a martial spirit everywhere. The art of karate was practiced and, I think, still has to be practiced that way today—in the same spirit as katana training. I really think Sensei Funakoshi would be very proud of all his students and how the art he brought to Japan from Okinawa is being practiced around world. However, it is important to distinguish three different stages in the development of shotokan karate—the Okinawan, the Japanese and that of Yoshitaka Funakoshi.

SPORT

I agree with the idea of karate becoming an Olympic sport. The sport aspect is a small part of the whole art—a small but important part nowadays. Karate competition is very fashionable these days and it has allowed the art to spread. In itself, that's not particularly bad but it may bring some consequences if we don't keep an eye on it. Competition might impoverish the art because practitioners tend to standardize the way they train, therefore creating a competition style. Fighters end up losing their personality and their training becomes competition-orientated. On the other hand, karate is not only budo, but budo is a big part of karate that has to be kept. It can be used to develop the human relationships. This is why the sportive side of karate is good. But it is only good as long as the techniques are kept in the right context and the karateka understand the tradition that links his spirit to the other parts of the art. I'd say that the sportsman has to respect the budo. It's important to keep the right attitude and approach to training while you develop the sport, but if you begin to modify the karate techniques in order to be better in sport competition—and you forget about the right zanchin, the right posture, and the right combat spirit—then sport karate will ruin real karate. Sport karate is useful during your youth but the art of karate is for all your life. Karate is karate, boxing is boxing, and tennis is tennis. You shouldn't modify techniques just to score a point. Your technique and spirit have to be strong, never lacking in concentration. I don't see a problem in doing sport competition and preserving the real spirit of karate in every technique you use in combat. This is the right way. You have to think about a life-or-death situation. Karate is a martial art which is practiced bare-handed. You try to render an opponent unable to fight by using a single technique.

JKA INSTRUCTORS COURSE

In the old days, the classes at the Instructor Course were very hard, very exhausting and tough. There was an unbelievable spirit in the air with Sensei Kanazawa, Sensei Shirai, Sensei Enoeda, et cetera. Classes today are very hard, but not that hard. After training there we were sent to different countries to teach the art of karate-do. I believe that JKA karate is the most researched and refined karate there is. The instructors training program allowed the students to devote themselves to the art, to completely immerse themselves in study and training. This is what made JKA karate so strong and the true reason why JKA teachers had such a high technical level. Many of us have been away from Japan for almost five decades! Our distancing from Japan meant we had to set our own standards—either to improve or deteriorate as karate-ka independently. We are always exchanging ideas and I believe our standard has greatly improved. I always look for reality training for myself and

my students. I like to analyze the technical and psychological levels of karate and the way it is expanding. I am daily searching for new techniques that are more relevant to the way I see the art these days. When karate was developing there were many gaps to be filled. Master Funakoshi knew that the influence of other methods was essential and that's why I'm trying to incorporate them. I truly believe in a healthy karate. Unfortunately, these days I see too much tension in the practitioners. They become so excited that they forget to relax their muscles. Trying hard is all they do and by the time they develop speed, their muscles are too tense. Therefore they can't relax properly in order to use their natural energy and muscle relaxation to build up speed in their techniques. Modern practitioners need to develop a sense of balance between the soft and hard side of karate.

KATA

For the beginners, kata is just a form, an external mold—but when you've trained for many years your understanding expands and kata becomes something else quite distinct. Also, you preferences in kata change with your age and evolution. It is the person's ability that causes the difficulty. Unfortunately, in most cases, the kata we see are not real. The judges in competition only look at rhythm. I believe everyone, including myself, should talk to each other about the different aspects related to kata. I think some people are losing the kata internal meaning just for competition purposes. And that's definitely something wrong.

MASATOSHI NAKAYAMA

Sensei Nakayama was a turning point in the evolution of the art and his dedication and work should be recognized by every practitioner around the world. He opened a lot of new doors for karate, not only for shotokan practitioners but for students of any karate style. Master Funakoshi was a true gentleman and the person taking over should be the same. Nakayama Sensei was a great man and a gentleman as well. Unfortunately, since he passed away the JKA has split and all the great teachers that once were together now are working in different directions. It's sad but there's not much you can do about it. The old top instructors like Sensei Nishiyama, Sensei Okazaki, Sensei Shoji, or myself—we are living out of Japan so a problem was created as far as choosing a leader.

PERSONAL EXPRESSION

I definitely do my own expression of the art. It depends on my body, my mentality, my spirit, and my attitude. It is based on the way I look at life itself. Everybody is different and after many years of practice and understanding of the principles of karate your own expression of what you have learned will see the light.. It takes many years of training and above all, a deep understanding of the fundamental principles of karate and yourself. I don't think the style is that important. For instance, Sensei Tagaki practices shotokai. The technique is different but the spirit is the same. The essence of the art is the same, it has not changed a bit. This is what is really important. I have a lot of friends that practice and teach other styles, and let me tell you that at a certain level it is not the art but the person that's important. The styles converge, they share the same principles but it's up to the practitioner to make it work. It's like playing piano; you can play Mozart or Chopin but if you are a lousy pianist, forget about it!

Egami Sensei for instance, developed the shotokai style, which seems strange to anyone practicing the more orthodox systems of karate-do. The kata are the same as shotokan but are performed in a soft, slow and fluid fashion, reminiscent of tai chi. Egami Sensei was one of the senior students of Master Funakoshi and he was an excellent technician. In fact, he was the model for the kata in the second edition of Funakoshi's book, *Karate Do Kyohan*. In the early '60s, Egami Sensei began his researches on the internal aspects of the martial arts and came upon his unique soft karate. He felt he was continuing his karate development in a way Funakoshi Gichin would have approved. He was an excellent karate-ka. Sensei Egami found something, but perhaps it was too difficult for him to transmit this to his students. He was very concerned with the "do" of karate-do.

CHANGES

I have changed a lot and the art has also changed. I guess all these changes have been for the good. I have been practicing karate for almost 50 years non-stop, every single day. But there is something that has not changed during all these years and that is the mentality and the training spirit found in Master Funakoshi's dojo. This spirit is still inside of me. From the technical point of view, the art of karate has greatly evolved over the years but I think that part of the old spirit has been lost. And that is not good. I believe that spirit has to be kept within the art because it is the real spirit of karate-do.

Make sure to rain hard, every single day. Always keep in mind the right spirit and attitude in training. Don't forget about striking a balance in training between kata and kumite because that is the real secret. I am very old but I still train as much as I can accordingly to my age. You never stop learning and this is something that you have to carve in your mind from the first day. From day one to the last day of your life you are always learning. In the end, it is not about the styles of karate—there is just karate. You make progress or you don't—you reach the standard or you don't. That's all. ◐

Shojiro

Koyama

I began training in Shotokan karate in 1950 at the age of 15. I attended Hosei High School in Tokyo. In my senior year, I became the captain of the school's karate team. In 1954, I entered Hosei University, where I trained under Master Saiki and Master Kimio Itoe. By the time of my graduation, I had become the Co-captain of the university's karate team, and I remained there as a team coach until 1964.

When I was young, I only studied and practiced my technique, and I thought that my technique would improve through this type of training. My instructors always said that I must also "Seek perfection of character" as part of my training and development or my technique would never really improve. Of course, as a youth I doubted that advice. I believed that "technique is simply technique." Now, however, I think I understand what my teachers were trying to tell me. After a lifetime of experience, I understand that hardship and struggle must be incorporated—in the form of character development—into one's training in order to improve one's performance.

My karate philosophy reflects my belief that under adverse circumstances and conditions of struggle, a person's true character emerges. This is true in life and in the microcosm of life that karate represents. For example, when a karateka is unsuccessful in a dan exam or tournament competition, his or her true nature is revealed quite clearly. Those people who have begun to understand the importance of character development understand that—when initially unsuccessful—patience and composure are most critical. Failure can be a very good learning experience. Many people do not understand this concept and are always quick to compliment and try to soften the blow when their student is unsuccessful. However, I believe that this soft approach will most often not bring out strength of character as efficiently as when one simply accepts failure, learns from it and commits to persevering despite of it. This mindset forms the core of educational karate and of karate as a lifetime exercise, and is, I believe, what is really meant by the first tenet of the shotokan dojo-kun: "Seek perfection of character."

Master Gichin Funakoshi wrote, "The ultimate aim of the art of karate lies not in victory or defeat, but in the perfection of character of its participants." He wrote this during the early 20th century, arguably the most aggressive and violent century in history. The generation of that time pioneered modern weapons of mass destruction and engaged in human rights violations of a scale never before seen or even imagined. Certainly, one would have hoped that the 21st century would bring a spiritual awakening and a fundamental change in

the nature of human relations as the world began to look back on the tragedies and violence of the previous era. Unfortunately, it seems that human relations remain very complicated. Although the world has had the opportunity to reflect on the possibilities that face the human race in an age in which technology is capable of vastly improving life, or conversely, destroying it. Sadly, aggressive regimes continue to threaten their citizens, nations continue to wage war and terrorists attack innocent civilians. Perhaps human nature is fixed and will never change. If this is the case, it certainly seems that society needs to pursue areas of spiritual growth or peace will continue to be elusive.

As Master Funakoshi explained, the value in the martial arts, such as karate, is to be found in the lessons learned from losing as well as winning. There are no true losers among practitioners of the martial arts, because both victory and defeat are opportunities for spiritual growth. Throughout life we must all learn to face both victory and defeat with grace and spiritual grounding. Otherwise, the disappointments of day-to-day living, over a lifetime, wear us down, make us bitter and cause us to behave aggressively, discourteously and possibly even destructively toward others. Karate fosters in us the ability to appreciate the learning opportunities inherent in defeat and loss throughout a lifetime of experiences, both good and bad.

One of the most important lessons that karate teaches us is that courtesy and respect are paramount. Without courtesy and respect, the martial arts are exactly the same as street fighting. That is what Master Funakoshi meant when he wrote the 20 basic precepts of karate, in which the very first one states that, "In karate, begin with a bow and finish with a bow." Where one consistently follows this principle, one begins to appreciate that courtesy and respect are more important than "winning." By respecting and valuing our opponents, we become capable of recognizing their courage, guts, mettle and spirit, regardless of who ultimately emerges "victorious." Character

development means recognizing that this "spirit" is far more important than the trophy or medal that the winner receives.

MASATOSHI NAKAYAMA

Master Nakayama was the essence of modern Budo. After WWII, Master Nakayama created a new Budo, which we still follow to this day. It used to be that there were no tournaments, just drilling in the basics with a one-punch, one-kill mindset, albeit confined to a non-tournament setting. This type of training appealed to only a limited number of people. Master Nakayama opened traditional karate to a much broader audience and a wider market of potential students with the advent of tournament karate. However, I think that Master Nakayama might look at the ultimate destination toward which karate seems to be headed and perhaps conclude that the sports mentality has been taken to an extreme. In that regard, as the father of modern karate, he might be a bit taken aback at the direction taken by some of his "children," a direction he probably never envisioned when he pioneered modern Budo.

Technique comes from the instructor's personality and personal philosophy. If your aim is to be strong and violent, all you need is technical competence, and philosophy is not important. But shotokan karate emphasizes the first principle of the dojo-kun: "Seek perfection of character." If your personal philosophy or behavior runs counter to the dojo kun, your technique will never really improve or reach its full potential. I already mentioned that when I was younger my instructor warned me that I was concerned with technique at the expense of attitude. I have since learned that if you improve and advance your mind (attitude), your technique will follow. Unfortunately, the reverse does not seem to be true. Personally, I recommend Zen training. Zen training focuses on good, correct posture and breathing. Of course, it is a bit dangerous when an instructor tries to teach Zen to others without first having personal instruction from an experienced leader or teacher. It is relatively easy to read a book and think that you understand the principles behind Zen. However, there can be some dangerous side effects to practicing the art improperly if you have not been correctly schooled in technique. Fortunately or unfortunately, students today seem to like sports karate. Therefore, a focus on basics is very important. Seventy percent of training should be in the basics but not only "basic" basics. Kihon with a partner in which application, coordination and practical elements of technique are emphasized is very beneficial.

I have a dream, a target destination if you will, but more important is right now, the present moment. Present life satisfaction and mental stimulation are very important. Without intellectual stimulation, a human being becomes like an animal … the spirit withers and the body soon dies. Training provides that source of stimulation. After every training session, I say, "Thank you God. I did it! Right in this moment I was able to do what I set out to do." Eventually, the little satisfactions and small moments of progress that come day by day will lead you to your goals and dreams, but today is all we ever really have. I always say that the dojo-kun is itself the practitioner's best defense. I don't really think about real fighting, and I believe that one should keep one's mind clear of thoughts about real-life enemies

and fighting when training. Your true opponent is your own mental limitation, not another person.

Early on I trained to be strong and to get stronger still. But now, through karate, I have come to understand how to be weak, how to recover from weakness, and how to maintain my level of skill and fitness. I have come to

understand and accept my weak side because I understand the importance of modesty and humility. Hard, challenging training helps cultivate modesty and humility, which naturally leads to a better understanding of the spiritual aspects of the martial arts. Therefore, keep training, don't give up and don't become discouraged by your moments of weakness. Instead, learn to value and cherish them for the ultimate spiritual growth that they will bring you. Ninety percent of life is composed of the ordinary and the mundane. An appreciation for the mundane is what is missing in today's karate training. For example, when I was a student at Hosei University in Japan, we had no tournaments … just basic dojo training. Our instructor would say, "Today we are going to do *heian shodan* 100 times." We would do it and be satisfied. Now, students always seem to be chasing the next big exciting event. Often, as a result, they have little patience for the type of ordinary practice and drilling that we did in the early days.

However, it is our responsibility as practitioners of lifetime educational karate to pass on the importance of the mundane aspects of life and training and to cultivate the patience that allows us to tap into the unconscious power of those mundane moments. Therefore, while tournaments are valuable and exciting, the more mundane events, such as the daily practice of basics and kata, are also important.

When I was young, I always felt fear. But as I have gotten older and entered the later stages of my life cycle, I am no longer really worried about anything. Why are people afraid? I believe it is because they have unhealthy desires such as more and more money and more and more popularity. The possibility of not obtaining these desires makes people nervous. I am approaching the end of my life's journey. I still have aims, plans and dreams, but these are no longer guided by unhealthy desires.

The most important quality of a successful karate-ka is commitment to everyday training and an appreciation of the mundane. Train hard, finish, bow and say "thank you" for the opportunity to sweat. The most important quality for a practitioner of lifetime karate is the ability to find such satisfaction in ordinary training. The successful practitioner of lifetime karate is successful because he has had a satisfying life, not because he is a tournament champion or 10th degree black belt. Satisfaction comes from ability to enjoy the ordinary and willingness to pass on one's wisdom as one ages.

I came to the United States more than four decades ago with a mission to spread Master Funakoshi's philosophy and teachings. That mission remains a work in progress, and I will never give up, no matter what circumstances may bring. It is my life's work, my passion and the *raison d'etre* for my dojo. I hope that you will make it your mission as well, so that we may pass the baton on to the next generation of karateka, and ensure that we and generations of the future may continue to benefit from the beauty that is Master Funakoshi's karate. ◉

Takayuki

Mikami

I joined the karate club as soon as I entered Hosei University. I was a little boy from a farm and Tokyo was a very tough city. I guess since I felt the need to build my confidence and improve my physical strength I decided to join the karate club. The first instructor I had was Mr. Saiki and then Mr. Kimio Ito. The training was very hard and there was a high level of dropouts, particularly during the first year.

We were happy to have the chance to leave Japan to spread karate around the world. It was like a mission to us. We were ready to give everything we had in training. We worked extremely hard in a very difficult time for Japan. We never looked for the easy life; our motivation for training was very, very different from the practitioners today. Also, it was a very important that we were allowed to constantly train—and this intensified our practice sessions. The JKA was well-regarded for its high technical level. For instance, after the instructor's program I kept training full time for another seven years! That's the reason why the JKA had such a great technical level compared to other schools and styles.

Today everything is different. The people training in Japan have to no plan to leave the country whatsoever. They don't need to go through the hard times and difficulties. This will definitely affect the future of the art. Technique-wise I believe it will be the same but as far as concerning the spirit, attitude, and philosophy it will not be.

JKA TRAINING

When I was in my fourth year at the university, Ito Sensei told me about entering the JKA to become an instructor. At the time they didn't have their own dojo or instructor program—everything was under construction. There were a lot of good karate-ka. Students from other universities joined the course, which helped to raise the training level. It is true that many dropped out and very few of us remained training at the new JKA dojo where Masatoshi Nakayama Sensei was the Chief Instructor. We used to do a lot of kihon—thousands of repetitions of each technique. Master Nakayama was a very tough instructor. The old training was very samurai-like. We used to drill, and drill, and drill without the instructors explaining anything.

If you didn't understand the technique, you did it 100 more times. You had to find it out by yourself. In Japan this way of teaching is called "teaching through the body."

It was very hard. It was comprised of two different parts; we, the students had to do all the work—I mean from cleaning the dojo to preparing the food, et cetera. Of course, we were being watched all the time, 24 hours a day, by our sen-pai. In the training aspect, don't forget that karate-ka from all over were anxious to check us out since we were receiving special training. Also some other groups and styles came to the JKA to challenge us. The sparring classes were very tough. It was free-sparring with no referee whatsoever.

GICHIN FUNAKOSHI

Unfortunately I never trained under Funakoshi Sensei. He was very old at that time but I saw him many times at the JKA head-quarters. He was always present at the belt test watching what you were doing. He was so old that he looked like a god to me.

A good instructor is not only a good technician. He must know how to teach a class, how to instill karate values, and how to deal with his student's psychology.

SPORT

People come to martial arts for several reasons and sport training is only around 10 percent. What we are seeing is a new karate born of a blend of Japanese tradition and Western customs and culture. Even in Japan many karate-ka call their teacher "coach" not "sensei." They conceive it more as sport. These days, karate has an sportive aspect, even the so-called traditional exponents go to tournaments and enjoy the sport. I don't think this is bad as long as we keep it in the proper perspective. Today, even the most traditional Japanese arts engage in contests. I don't think competition has to interfere with the traditional principles of the art. Winning or losing is not the most important thing in competition. The sport competition teaches us a lot of thing that can't be learned in the dojo such as pressure in front of people, mental control in an strange environment, et cetera. But you have to keep the right perspective.

PHILOSOPHY

The Japanese philosophy and the Western philosophy are different. Maybe the goal is the same but the approach definitely is not.

The Western practitioner in a final match will jump and celebrate after scoring a point. In the true spirit of budo, you must concentrate and stay calm and focused, keeping all your emotions under control. This allows you to develop energy while exerting control over the ego. In the West, the karate-ka build their energy using their ego. Doing it this way is a very easy method to get a big head. And once you lose your spirit it is very difficult to get it under control again.

MY KARATE

I'm proud I never changed my direction in karate. I don't care about all the difficulties and hard times I went through, I always got self-satisfaction and spiritual development by keeping the same path throughout my life. Sometimes when I got bored I kept doing the same basic things over and over again until I reached a new level. I believe that communication can help you to find your own way. I also believe the one must be honest and sincere, putting 100 percent into everything you do because without effort nothing is gained. Karate is about effort and sacrifices. It is true that sometimes we make mistakes but we must always make a real effort.

KATA AND KUMITE

Kata and kumite are two parts of the same whole. I know some people think they don't need kata in their quest to be great fighters but they are wrong. This is an incorrect approach to karate. The student has to dedicate the same amount of time to both aspects but keep in mind that kata needs a very in-depth study. The analysis of one single kata may take years; by this I mean the different uses of the same technique, and its application in kumite and self-defense. I recommend to study deeply one or two kata, although you can get a lot of knowledge and inspiration by learning others as well. Kata teaches the correct body positioning, the proper execution of the techniques, focus, balance, et cetera. One gains powerful techniques from correctly using the body. Why do you think the best kata people are the best fighters? Unfortunately, practitioners today rely too much on their own physical power instead of learning proper form and technique.

Funakoshi Sensei changed all the Okinawa kata to better fit into his conception of shotokan karate. Originally, the stances were narrower and higher, but JKA changed to deeper and lower positions in order to increase the difficulty and improve the training methods to achieve better physical development. The original stances were made for fighting but since the purpose no longer holds they adapted karate to the present day, looking for a better overall physical development.

HIROKAZU KANAZAWA

My legendary fight against Kanazawa Sensei was the hardest match I ever fought in my life! We knew each other very well since we sparred in the dojo all the time. I was aware of his longer reach so I had to be very careful while trying to break through his guard. He was cautious about my speed so he didn't want to close the distance improperly. After a while we were very tired, both physical and mentally. Concentration was a key factor. A lot of people from my home-

town of Nigata where watching, including my family. Kanazawa Sensei had support from his family as well. Neither one of us wanted to disgrace or disappoint our families. I realized that Kanazawa was thinking the same way. So I said, "Why should I give up?" I knew that I had to use all my speed to score on Kanazawa since he is a strong fighter. We faced each other for four overtime periods, stalking each other and seeking that deci-

sive psychological moment to launch the final attack. But that attack never came. There was nothing left in our bodies. Only our spirits kept us fighting. Finally, we were both were declared champions. It is the only time this has ever occurred.

TRADITIONAL

In real traditional karate if you had to fight, you would kill and you can't do that today. So what do people mean by traditional? Traditional karate is not about technique like the people like to describe, it is about attitude. It's about life or death and not about doing *hikite* when you punch *gyaku-tsuki*. I guess karate has lost some of its essence. It was originally for self-defense but the demands changed with the times. We were trained based on the fact one was a warrior.

SHU-HA-RI

Your body changes so the way you do things has to change. Not the inner principles behind the motion, but certain aspects of it. I started to modify some things according to my body when I was 50. Shotokan is a great style but it is very difficult for older people. It is important to find ways of adapting the methods without losing the

principles. Unfortunately, power and speed in techniques is over-emphasized and a lot of karate techniques do not need that much power or speed. As your joints start to hurt, you need more effective, practical techniques. It is very important for the practitioner to be aware of the *shu-ha-ri* principle which is the normal way of the martial arts in Japan. First you strictly train under your teacher and you imitate without questioning—*shu*. Then comes *ha*, where you master the physical techniques and gain your own insight into the nature of the art, spirit, and techniques and incorporate these insights into your daily practice. Finally, after many years comes *ri*, where you separate from your instructor and go out on your own.

FUTURE

Sometimes karate is boring and I understand. Everything is boring if you do it everyday for 30 or 40 years! The secret lies in not giving up, but in training the simple things until you feel better. That's the real test of budo. The hardest thing to teach in martial arts is spirit, but it is the most important aspect the art of karate can offer to its practitioners. The mental and spiritual aspects of the martial arts can help one to overcome any kind of difficulties.

Masatoshi
Nakayama

Budo has always been part of my family. My grandfather belonged to the Sanada clan of Samurai. My father was a disciplinarian since he was a military man. As far as my training, I did kendo before entering Takushoku University. I always wanted to visit China and Takushoku was the best university for getting training and education to work and teach overseas. So I secretly took and passed the entrance examination.

I already had kendo training so I looked for a kendo class at Takushoku. I checked the training schedule and I misread the timetable and showed up at a class where everybody was wearing white uniforms! I had read a little bit about karate and all those movements were kind of amusing so I decided to sit there and watch. Suddenly, one of the men approached me and challenged me to try it and I did. Very soon I realized that it was not as simple as I thought. That day I had my first challenge of trying to perfect the karate movements—and I still have that feeling of wanting to perfect karate inside of me.

53

GICHIN FUNAKOSHI

Sensei Funakoshi always kept a very strict discipline inside and outside the dojo. Karate-do was a way of life for him, not something to be left behind when you left the dojo. The training under him was very hard and demanding; the classes consisted of long hours of performing each technique hundred of times. Kata was repeated 50 or 60 times and makiwara training was done until our hands bled. Master Funakoshi used to join us for makiwara training and hit the post with his elbow thousands of times. He seemed to enjoy that particular aspect of training.

Training and traveling with him allowed me to see the man he was from many perspectives. For instance, he always seemed to be in a constant state of vigilance, no matter where he was. This made a big impression on me. Many times he did things to teach me that I was still young and immature and that I needed more self-discipline and self-restraint because those aspects are where true courage lies. He showed me that it takes more courage to walk away from a fight than to get into one. He was a visionary who was able to see that the students—who mainly came from kendo and judo, where sparring was a usual aspect of training—needed sparring in karate-do training. He

devised sets of five-step sparring sequences the students could practice in a more combative environment than the techniques of kata. Don't forget at that time we only had kata and kihon as methods of training. Of course some of the students were hot blooded, and if you failed to counter-attack at the right time they would hit you right away without waiting for you.

In the early days of karate-do, for some years after 1935, college karate clubs all over Japan held inter-school matches. They were called *kokangeiko*, which translate as "exchange of courteous practice." The participants freely attacked each other with all the karate techniques at their disposal, and the original purpose was to promote friendship between clubs, not to beat anybody up. For instance, one person attacked only once. Then his opponent counterattacked, again just once. They continued in strictly controlled alternation. But sometimes, the young blood of the students ran too hot to be satisfied with such tameness. They could not resist the temptation to use to the fullest the techniques they had learned and the powers they had gained through daily training at the dojo. There would be five or six contestants from each university in these freestyle matches. If something happened or went out of control, it was the responsibility of the judges to step in and part them. The truth is, the judges rarely had time to exercise their responsibility. Some of the contestants had broken teeth or twisted noses. Others had earlobes nearly ripped off or were paralyzed from a kick to the belly—the injured crouching here and there around the dojo—it was a bloody scene. It was tough.

Master Funakoshi often recited an old Okinawan saying: "Karate is the art of virtuous men." Needless to say, for students of karate to thoughtlessly boast of their power or to display their technique in scuffles goes against the soul of karate-do. The meaning of karate-do goes beyond victory in a contest of mastery or self-defense techniques.

CHINESE MARTIAL ARTS

I started training in Chinese martial arts in 1937 when I was sent as an exchange student to study Chinese language and history. To be totally honest, I was not impressed by the Chinese methods of fight-

ing because they emphasized circular movements and at first sight they seemed to lack focus. But after training with several teachers my opinion started to change. I studied mainly under an old teacher called Sifu Pai, of a northern style. He was really good with his legs and his defensive actions were marvelous . Since the northern styles emphasize the use of the legs, I developed two new kicks. One was the pressing block with the sole of the foot *taisoku uke*, or with the lower shin, *haisoku uke*, and the other was the reverse roundhouse kick, *ura mawashi geri*. These techniques were added to shotokan later in 1946 when I returned to Japan and, of course, with the permission of Sensei Funakoshi.

JKA

A friend of mine had a great relationship with the head of the Japanese Ministry of Education. The ban of karate was not lifted until 1948, and in 1949 Sensei Funakoshi had a meeting to discuss the martial arts and the future of karate after the war. It was in that meeting that the nucleus of the JKA was formed and I was put in charge of the technical standards for the new organization. In 1955, the JKA was incorporated as an educational body under the Ministry of Education. We had to come up with the technical and grading standards to be registered with the Ministry of Education. Under the total supervision of Sensei Funakoshi I began to formulate the instructor program. I received great help from other karate-ka such as Teruyuki Okazaki, Hidetaka Nishiyama and Motokuni Sugiura. In 1957, after the death of Sensei Funakoshi, I was elected the Chief Instructor of the Japan Karate Association. In 1958 the JKA was declared an official body by the Japanese government and we made a great effort to unify many of the other shotokan karate schools in Japan.

ADDITIONAL KATA

Sensei Mabuni was a very respected karate-do master and Gichin Funakoshi had high respect for him. He was a living encyclopedia of kata from many different sources. Sensei Funakoshi took me with him to visit Sensei Mabuni and he told me to learn two kata from him—*ninjushijo* and *gojushijo*—so we could study them later on in detail and more carefully. Eventually, we changed the format to specifically suit the structure of the shotokan method, conforming the movements that are not practiced by our members. Gichin Funakoshi wanted to grasp the essence of the different karate-do styles and incorporate them into his method. It's important to remember that these kata were added to the basic 15 kata that Funakoshi taught. For instance, his son Yoshikata, went to Okinawa and returned with *sochin*. All these additions definitely improved the art and never in any way changed the basic concept of the karate taught by Sensei Funakoshi.

SPORT

The practitioner needs to learn how to overcome anxiety and how far he should stand from an opponent. Without practice against an opponent, we cannot have the chance to work at our greatest capacity. Fighting is dangerous, but fighting is indispensable. Only through it can we maintain the essential skills of karate. Once I organized a match with the contestants wearing protective gear, but the special clothing was an

obstacle and turned out to be itself the cause of unexpected injuries. I had to keep looking for a solution. That was just before the beginning of World War II.

After the war, even Japan abandoned the militarism of the past and made a fresh start as a nation based on pacifism. The college karate clubs kept holding their wild fighting contests, and the number of injured kept mounting. In the new climate of peace, violence in any form was a hateful thing and not accepted in the society. If karate remains as it was, I thought, it will be regarded as the embodiment of violence and will eventually fade away. Yet judo and kendo were developing as sports. The glorious contests of swimmers and baseball players were brightening the postwar gloom. Young karate practitioners began to hope that karate would become a sport, and in order to do that it would have to have rules for matches.

I'm still afraid of one thing, however. As karate matches become popular, and they are these days, the karate practitioners become too absorbed in winning. It is easy to think that gaining a point matters most, and matches are likely to lose the very essence of karate. Karate matches are degenerating into mere exchanges of blows. Moreover, I cannot say whether the idea of free-fighting styles matches the soul of karate as taught by Master Funakoshi, the founder of karate-do. The soul of his karate requires quite a high standard of ethics. And we can't ever forget that.

PHILOSOPHY

The soul of karate-do is the wish for harmony among people. Such harmony is based on courtesy, and it is said that the Japanese martial ways begin with courtesy and end with courtesy. Karate, if practiced properly, can be used as self-defense and a sport without

losing its essence. If the principles are taught properly it won't matter what the practitioner is doing—he will be doing "karate-do." The art has to be used to develop the person and it's when the student trains only for competition when the direction is wrong. The secret is to train "in the art," not "in the sport." We must train with a balance in our minds. Competition karate has to maintain the idea of *ikken hisatsu*, which will keep the seriousness of true budo and not simply allow the sportive scoring of points. If we do this, karate-do will keep its essence as an art and will be practiced by people of all ages, because is not simply a sport but a complete art used to develop the whole individual. The art of karate-do is about daily practice and if you follow this, the real truth will come to you because life is the same as karate training—a daily and constant practice. ◉

Hidetaka
Nishiyama

I started training in karate around 1943. Karate was not popular at that time, but judo and kendo were. I did them because martial arts training was incorporated into the school system. But I liked them very much, so it was not a problem for me. I heard about karate and I got interested. Unfortunately, I had to look all over Tokyo but finally found Mr. Toyama's dojo. I began my training there and a lot of people began telling me that I should go to Mr. Funakoshi's dojo. I stayed with Mr. Toyama for over a year-and-a-half and then I went to Master Funakoshi's school. Remember that it was wartime—all the senior instructors were away at the war. So mostly at the university we saw only Master Funakoshi and Master Kuriyama. I did train sometimes with Master Funakoshi's son, Yoshitaka. He was young and very strong. I remember that all the young students were trying to copy him. Master Funakoshi's techniques were in principle the same as Yoshitaka's, but the external form was different. I guess some of the youngest students didn't understand that, since they were only looking at the external form.

The number of karate practitioners was very small because the war created a big blank in the instructor's ranks. Karate was an almost unknown martial art. That's why it was so difficult to find a dojo— only in three or four universities could you find one.

After the war, I was the captain of the university team and we started a rotation training in different university dojo because almost everybody had forgotten their kata. People who had studied for a long time couldn't remember, so we all had to get together, use our information, old reading materials, and our personal experiences. We also used to gather to train under Master Funakoshi.

The older practitioners felt they were more traditional, and in the university there was a little bit of class distinction, so some egos came out. Then we decided to start the Japan Karate Association. I recall that we had no dojo so we still rotated around the universities. Without a central dojo, things were no as smooth as they should have been. Master Hironishi was very good in bringing people together but later on he decided, along with some other shotokan schools, to form the shotokai.

TRAINING

In the early days, we didn't practice many techniques or combinations. No variety at all. One hour *kiba-dachi* (horse stance), 1,000 punches, 1,000 kicks, and pretty much that was it! Sometimes we would repeat the same kata a hundred times in a row. We had this kind of training all the time. The first day I went to class, my teacher showed

me the kiba-dachi stance and left me there for an hour! The instructors did not teach with a lot of explanations. The student had to pick up things for themselves and to do so they had to study their master's daily life—how he worked, how he lived, how he expressed himself in different circumstances. After three or four years, the master would decide to start teaching techniques, but without much detail—maybe just a few special points. They never liked coaching or teaching scientifically. You had to find out for yourself the right way, just by feeling the technique. And of course, you were never supposed to ask questions.

Fortunately, for many, these days there is more teaching, more explanations, and more help on the instructor's part. Curiously, the principles are the same, they haven't changed. We have new ideas and training methods but the fundamental principles are the same. Sometimes I wonder how the old masters knew about the right physics and dynamics of the human body. The principles of all styles are the same. Goju-ryu, shito-ryu, shotokan, wado-ryu, et cetera, all share the same basic principles. It just happens that the explanations are a little bit different and the form looks different. For instance, goju-ryu uses short movements since it was devised for short distance fighting. They look for developing strong muscle power for close range techniques. Shotokan put more emphasis on wider movements and dynamic body actions—getting the power more from rotation and body shifting.

What it is true in any style is the fact that regardless of the style, every karate-ka needs to know how to develop power in short range and long range using strong muscle actions and contractions. We must think how to make power in different ways. All the actions must start

from the floor for external force. This is the very basic principle of momentum and as Newton mentioned in his lst, 2nd and 3rd laws, without an external force you never increase energy and momentum. It has to be remembered that all the actions in karate are from the floor. I practice shotokan, but shotokan is not the only karate. We must never think shotokan is complete or that shotokan is the best.

JKA INSTRUCTORS COURSE

Taiji Kase was a student of Sensei Hironishi and Hirokazu Kanazawa and Sensei Mikami were among the first people to graduate from the Instructor's School. That was around 1957 or 1958. I remember that I met Sensei Kase and Sensei Sugiura just after I graduated from Takushoku University. Mr. Sugiura is a very nice person and very serious about everything he does. I recall that Mr. Kase was working for a company at that time but that we always found time to get together for training. These great karate-ka continued training and studying—they never stopped. They always looked for their own personal development. That's the reason they are so good. Look at instructors such as Enoeda, Shirai, and Kanazawa. They were very young men when I first met them as the chief of the JKA instruction department. There were many instructors who were at the same level as them, even better than them, and with more and better understanding of the principles. At that time they were not so special. But these other instructors did not continue their development and quit. Conversely Enoeda, Kanazawa, and Shirai dedicated their life to the art of karate. You have to keep studying and training for self-development in the art if you really want to reach a very high level.

During the beginnings of the Instructors Course at the honbu dojo, I used to put on a white belt and go into the Instructors School classes. I did it to see if I could learn *gyaku-tsuki* or *kiba-dachi*. I tried to think just like a beginner and I took notes about the instructor's performance and teaching ability—then I brought it up in the course. I know it was very difficult for the new instructors but it was also for me. I knew that I had to do it so I could find out by personal experience if the beginners were receiving their instruction properly. After all, that's what karate-do is all about—personal experience.

To me it's sad to see how many good karate-do practitioners ignore how to coach or instruct in a professional way. It is not enough for the teacher to demonstrate the technique and for the students to repeat it in the old way. We must advance more in order to progress.

PERSONAL EXPRESSION

Karate-do provides an excellent all-around exercise to develop coordination and agility by using all body muscles in a very balanced way. As a self-defense method, and through the training and use of the principles and knowledge of the art, the student is prepared to both physically and mentally defend himself against any attack. Of course, the sport is important but only if we follow the precepts of the art and we don't forget the

65

very essence of it. On other hand, karate is art not science. It is an art that uses scientific principles. Science doesn't make karate. Personally—and because I learned my karate from the feel of the techniques—I think no science can explain this feeling. It can only explain the way the movements are done and the physical science behind the movements. All traditional karate is one—karate-do. Traditional karate is budo. We must keep this philosophy. We must continue developing new teaching methods to give the next generation the best possible karate. This is our responsibility as leaders.

I always say that you have to develop you own way, but this is where scientific explanations of each movement come in. If you copy Picasso or Van Gough or Monet, this might be OK just as a means for learning. When you look at the work of these masters you see art at its highest level. They didn't change the art, they were art. That's the difference.

Every karate practitioner has a different body. Through training and understanding kata in the right way, they seek their final form—they

become their own masters for expressing karate. The principles are there and they come out naturally. The good karate master teaches his students to find their own way, not to follow his. Students that venture out on their own too soon, or without the right amount of knowledge and understanding, will never know what they're doing. In martial arts there is not a "set logic," everything is a matter of experience.

MASATOSHI NAKAYAMA

I felt tremendously sorry when we lost Nakayama Sensei. I always felt that karate needs peo-

ple like him to reach higher stages of development.
He worked very hard
until the last day of his life
giving seminars, lectures,
coaching at the university,
giving demonstrations, et
cetera. During the war he
went to China to research
karate's roots. What is
more, he took his wife
and two children along.
He was a big influence in
my life. I can only say that
Sensei Nakayama devoted
his life to the promotion
of karate-do.

SPORT

Competition is good but only while keeping the real values of traditional karate. Don't forget that karate-do is based on the art of self-
defense. In karate there is something called "*todome*" or "finishing
blow." It is very similar to the idea in the old fencing schools of killing
the opponent with only one action. I'm not against sport, but the problem with modern competition is that you don't need to feel budo. In
real karate, if you miss your block you are going to get hurt. There's no
second chance. This state of mind changes your whole conception of
what you're doing in kumite. You must pay much more attention to
your training. If there's no contact in sport karate, why train the kihon?
You don't need power! The punch might make contact and the fighter
score the point, but in a real situation, there is no damage! For me, this
is not karate and I believe that the sport side is growing a lot and the
spiritual and budo side is going down.

KATA

Kata is karate. All karate techniques are taken from kata. Let me put it this way: if you look at the history of karate, all the old masters developed certain katas based on their perception of combat. Original kata is very valuable. What some people don't understand is that while they were going through this research, they found out the very essence of movement in the body. What they did was to understand the principle behind the physical motion, and its relationship with the body, and use it in the application of the technique. In the old days, we never referred to kata as form, as we understand it today. Kata used to mean "symbol," although it was written in the same way. The physical movement was just a vehicle to understand and identify the internal principle. Only after that did they began to apply the technique. It is very important to teach these aspects in the right way, with the complete spiritual dimension that is called in Japanese "fudoshin."

The practitioner must first study the kata at the outside form, but seek the principles. Kata is like saying "for example." Later on the student must connect the principle to the application. The old masters experienced these applications. Therefore, the practitioner has to study the outside form first, then understand the principle, and later on connect the principle to the actual application. Unfortunately, many teachers and students have decided to change the outside form right away. You must study and understand—not just look at the outside form which is just an example. The old masters would first study the outside actions of the kata then digest it. They would make the

kata their own, but not by changing the techniques and movements, but making it match their own body.

Kata is the symbol of karate so it never changes. Unfortunately, 95 percent of the people don't understand kata meaning—only the outside movements which are irrelevant without understanding. Each kata evolved out of the experience of the masters. Through it, they embody the principles of karate. The good student has to learn through careful imitation and endless practice. This is the traditional way, not only for karate but even for other things like flower arranging, for instance. The student must copy the designs for a long time and, in the end, once he has picked up the principles, develop his own way. ◐

Tsutomu
Ohshima

Funakoshi Sensei was teaching at Waseda University. At that time, he was already an old man and we had to carry him up the stairs to the dojo and then back down again after class. I believe he was in his 80s.

Before the war, the Japanese were very proud of our traditions and cultural beliefs. Not only in the martial arts but also society in general. We believed that our samurai were the best fighting men in the world, but the atomic bomb changed many things. Japanese society was shocked, and we were to believe that foreign technologies were stronger.

During the 1950s, right after WW II, the Japanese thought that going to America was best. We lost respect for what we had and the new generations accepted a more materialistic attitude. They began to copy Western ways of behaving and thinking. I saw that after the war. My countrymen no longer respected their own culture, and immediately I felt that there was something that had to be saved. I came to the U.S. and soon questioned why people who had the opportunity of playing all these games—football, baseball, basketball—wanted to learn the martial arts from me. Some of my friends told me that we

should try to change karate into a sport to make it more appealing to the masses! But I never wanted to do that because tradition and the ethics of Budo would be lost and practice would have no other meaning than trying to beat someone else. My idea was to show the American people through karate-do that our culture was a second-class thing and that it was a serious and intellectual activity. In 1955, people didn't really know what to expect from karate classes. They viewed them as a hobby, something to give them a sense of what Japanese culture was all about. The United States of America and the Western world have tremendous potential power. All human societies have. Our enemy is not some other place. Our enemy is in our own minds. We always have to project improvement for ourselves. This is what all these great people throughout history have taught. This is what the martial arts teach. This is what the Bible teaches.

It's important to face yourself directly, strictly and honestly. That philosophy has had a very strong impact on my life. At one point, I thought that I was OK. When I started to look at myself through different eyes, I realized that I'm full of weakness and cowardice. That gave me more reasons to push myself. So, what is the karate philosophy? I think it is when you face yourself and are honest.

People think that someone is a loser because nobody follows him or because nobody recognizes him. For example, I have always tried real hard and done everything straight, but that type of lifestyle is not always interesting to other people. That can be disappointing and frustrating. The general public does not always care about quality or depth. They want to take the easy way out and go with the flashy things. For me, however, I want someone to remember me in 200 years. Of course, I will not be here. But when people talk about me, I want them to say that this guy was OK. He did a good job. He tried somehow. I realize, of course, that 99 percent of the people are not going to care about the human mind or show any interest. Again, that is alright. That does not hurt me. I am not looking to be popular. I just want to try my best.

A humble person often comes across the same as a person who has an inferiority complex, but that doesn't mean he has the complex. Second, a person with confidence has no need to hurt anyone. Why? Because he has confidence. Next, if a person without any confidence gets a position of power, money or strength, he will become cruel, mean and bad. On the other hand, if a person with confidence and humility gets the same position, he will not be this way. These philosophies do not apply just to the martial arts. There is actually no connection. I am not a moralist. Now, let's think about a period of time from the ancient days until today. If a selfish, mean, nasty guy survived [some ordeal], everyone would look up to him. He would be [considered] a winner. The martial arts show, however, that that type of men-

tality is a weakness. What kind of human being is a real winner? A genuine human being. It's very clear. If a genuine human being cannot be a winner, I would have quit a long time ago.

When someone else does something wrong, we don't forgive him. However, when we do something wrong, it's OK and we expect others to forgive us. That is ugly, stupid, immature

or a sign of a weakness of the human mind. So, when I talk about facing yourself with strict eyes, I'm talking about making yourself stronger every day. Can you do this without being selfish and without forgiving someone every day? You can't. Of course, we try, and so do I. But I am not successful every day. It's important, however, that we try really hard.

There are many kinds of individuals on the earth and they all have the right to live equally, but the truth is that not all are equal. Some are mature, and some are immature. Education plays an important part on how an individual will be when grows up. Usually, when we get older, we become more selfish and greedy, with no time or energy for others. It is important to have a good educational system that doesn't spoil the young generation. Everybody wants to lead, but a leader has to be a first-class human being. He can stand by himself and work hard, but he cannot do everything for himself. He has to do things for others. In the martial arts, we are racing toward a situation in which we will see who can be the strictest with himself. The martial arts contribute to human society in this way. We are racing toward who can be the strictest with himself and honest with himself. This was the original idea in the martial arts. Unfortunately, many people don't get this message. In the old times, this was the most important idea in Budo ... reach a higher level and become a strong

human being. But strong doesn't mean big arms; it means who can be a more strict human being with himself. That is the idea of the martial arts, and that is the essence of Budo.

For instance, when you clean the place where you train, you are showing appreciation and respect to the place that gives you a chance to practice. Don't forget that polishing the floor is in fact the art of polishing your own mind. Karate is

Photo courtesy of T. Muzila

a crystal of the human spirit and its heritage is a gem I intend to preserve. We are all trying to get out from underneath our stupidity, blindness, weakness and cowardice. We must open our heart to the right way to act.

My black belts know that what they are learning is not for appearance or just for the use of competition or self-defense, but for their own spirit and soul … for their lives. They have learned to recognize their own imperfections and ugliness. They can be proud of it, because it is not an easy task. In the world, there are good people and dishonest people. What is important is that good people don't give up to the crooked people. One little stone in a big lake makes a ripple that spreads out very far, and that's what we try to do in the martial arts. What is the essence of this? To end the ugliness and selfishness in the world, we have to cut out our own ugliness and selfishness first.

A successful individual in our modern society is someone who has a lot of money and properties. "He is a successful person," they say when the see a millionaire. But what they don't realize is that there is

no connection between the material things that person has and his mental maturity. There are many immature and lucky "successful" people in the world. In terms of success in the Western world, I am not successful at all. But I am successful in my terms because I have good members and good friends who trust me very much. So I am quite happy. I never have any troubles of my own, nor do my members who have been practicing seriously for many years. Everything I have belongs to my students. It is not mine, regardless of how expensive the things surrounding me may be. My students gave them to me.

KATA

Let's say that one teacher creates a kata. Years later, 20 of his students create another 20 new forms; by the next generation, there are more than 1,000 kata! This makes no sense. How can I change what I was taught by Funakoshi Sensei? I don't think he ever considered what he taught as some kind of style or school. The fundamental element of shotokan is that we try to be strict with ourselves because there is no limit to what we can accomplish. We must be straight and honest with ourselves. This is the tradition of Funakoshi Gichin.

Before he went to Tokyo from Okinawa, Funakoshi Sensei visited and trained with many masters to learn their forms. I assume that maybe he learned 60 or 80 kata, but I believe that he probably didn't spent many hours on each of them. The idea, as Funakoshi Sensei showed in the later years of his life, is that it is nonsense to memorize dozens of kata. It is ridiculous. He never told me this, but his teachings were in that direction. In the Western world, the people think that if you know 60 kata, you are better than the practitioner who knows only 30. And that is wrong. This exemplifies a process of accumulation in which the truth is that true Budo and true karate are just the opposite. It is about simplification. We have to simplify, simplify and simplify what we do. Quality in our acts, not quantity. Quality in our kata, not quantity of forms. If you know 20 kata, then make 10 better. If you only know 10, make five extremely good. Even five is too many for a true Budo-ka. Put yourself into the kata. Make the form 10,000 times. Then, when you think you have grasped the essence, go back and repeat it another 50,000 times. Only when you reach the threshold of repeating a kata 150,000 times can you start to think that the kata is yours.

The idea is to become one with what you do, with the kata, with the physical movement. You express your best with all of your energy. That is the direction of the true karate. And kata training is for

Photo courtesy of T. Muzila

that. To invent a new kata to impress a bunch of people is not karate
… it is being a Hollywood star.

ZEN

In the arts of Budo, there is the experience of the total moment.
When you are waiting on an opponent or waiting for an attack, your
mind is empty, your body is awake and totally relaxed, and you experience something that can't be put in words, simply because it has
nothing to do with words. It is experience. During meditation, you
come into contact with a feeling that is much more than just a cultural treasure and more than just an ability to fight. Of course, the
martial arts are very related to Shintoism, so I'm very fond of that
study. I have been strongly influenced by Zen, and every night, no
matter where I go, no matter how late I stay out, I never miss my sitting in meditation. Zen meditation was important to the samurai
about 800 years ago. They called it the martial arts of moving Zen.
When we get excited, we move around, but we hope that our mentality is clean and calm like the Pacific Ocean is today. We want to
feel the same thing before and after. After WW II, about 1945, I went
to Japan. The people were struggling, and many were trying to cut off
the traditional mentality, such as Zen. Many said that was junk.

I'm an old man who is 70 years old. An opponent could destroy me within a few minutes. I know in my mind, however, that I've got to face this guy, and it could be a fight for my life. What I feel is strong, and I will go into it [the encounter] with an open mind. I feel that way. I will forget my age; I will forget that my body has a herniated disc and I will forget that my legs will not move like they once did. I do not know how to resolve this, but I'm ready to make the best of it right now. I will make my fists right now and maybe the technique will follow. For me, it is like that.

I want to live comfortably without money. That's enough for me. I make my best and my members make their best. And though I won't have a chance to see it, it makes me happy to think that maybe after 200 years somebody will still be practicing karate here where I have taught. ☻

Teruyuki

Okazaki

Master Nakayama led the classes while Master Funakoshi would sit down and tell Nakayama Sensei what to do. He was always there observing. Master Funakoshi always stressed five important points in his teachings: the mental aspects, the physical aspects, staying calm, being exact, and being natural. He liked to explain how the human body works and how important it was to use the correct techniques to attack the right body parts.

Master Funakoshi never said that we should copy his form because he understood that his body weight and his body-type made the stances and the form of the techniques that way. He was a very scientifically-minded person—don't forget that he was a school teacher. He developed the physical techniques in a certain way but he used to say, "Don't copy. Judge it by your body type." It is very difficult to explain his movements. They looked almost without power, and more like a beautiful ballet.

Master Funakoshi enjoyed very much being with Master Mifune of judo, Master Morihei Ueshiba of aikido, and Master Nakayama of kendo. They used to give demonstrations together. He always said to us that he respected very much Master Jigoro Kano's thinking of the

martial arts. I know Master Kano helped Master Funakoshi when he started to teach the art of karate in Japan.

I remember that every time we passed in front of the Kodokan, Master Funakoshi always took off his hat and bowed. "He's my teacher," he used to say. "Of course," we all answered, "but he's judo." And Master Funakoshi replied, "It doesn't matter, a martial art is martial art and I must respect it!"

Master Funakoshi's last years were taken up with instruction and preparation to send instructors all over the world. In 1953 we did a nationwide US tour for judo and karate.

GICHIN FUNAKOSHI

There was no "shotokan" style. Master Funakoshi just called it karate-do because he wanted it to be called karate-do. But out of respect his students started calling it "shoto" which it was Master Funakoshi's pen name. At that time, we did not have any style. We were practicing karate-do.

The training was very hard, very difficult. The training sessions were up to six hours each day, six days a week. We would stand in *kiba-dachi* and punch for two hours in the morning. Then, the same for another two hours in the afternoon and for another two hours in the evening. Most people just gave up. The next three months were dedicated to kicking—just kicking techniques. After six or seven months of this kind of training, they started to combine both aspects and kata training was incorporated into the classes and became the focal point. This kind of training built up our muscles to an extraordinary degree. Our arms and legs were really powerful. But I didn't understand that back then. It took me over a year to see that the more hard work I put into my training the more benefits I got from it. If I missed one training session I didn't feel good at all—not my body, not my mind.

MASATOSHI NAKAYAMA

Master Nakayama wanted us to train under other karate masters, that's why he used to invite Gogen Yamaguchi from goju-kai and Hinori Otshuka from wado-ryu to teach us a different approach to the art. All these instructors gave lectures on their methods of karate and taught us various kata. I really think this was an excellent approach to help us better understand the complete art of karate-do.

My generation was very fortunate to have trained under Funakoshi Sensei and to have been led by Nakayama Sensei, but I guess that no one considers themselves good enough to do the job we have to do. We were educated to believe in high quality karate-do, both technically and spiritual-ly. This is the only way karate can be passed down to future generations.

I would like to see what Nakayama Sensei suggested before passing away—the Budo Olympics. All budo arts together, exchanging techniques and training methods where there are no winners or losers. This would return us to the original concept of budo and we could educate people about the art and the true meaning of the Way of the Warrior. Nakayama Sensei

said to me, "We must make people understand the true martial arts way." And this is what I'm trying to do, and the very reason why even after a tournament we still do the dojo-kun.

Nakayama Sensei was like a father to me—sometimes like an older brother who was always there helping me and guiding me. Master Funakoshi was like a grandfather. I must fulfill my obligation to my original teachers. Karate-do was taught by Master Funakoshi and Master Nakayama as a way of life. He gave us, his proteges, the *Shoto Ni Ju Kun* or 20 Precepts To Live By. The idea of those is that karate-do is budo and its goal is to develop character in human beings and to avoid conflicts.

JKA

The Japan Karate Association was officially organized around 1955. I was hired as an assistant instructor and quit the job I had. I became the first coach at the instructor's course. Master Nakayama had plans to make official instructors and I became a kind of guinea pig, because he used to give me several projects to study, practice and report on. He analyzed everything I gave him and later on he started the official instructors program. The idea was that becoming a karate

instructor was to be the equal of studying the curriculum in a university to become a teacher. We had courses on how to teach the techniques, how to practice by yourself, and on subjects like physics, scientific aspects, et cetera. One of the prerequisites was a degree from a 4-year college. So this course became sort of a Master's degree.

Karate-do is budo and budo is not a sport. The real meaning of budo is to go into life more deeply and improve physical and spiritual qualities through hard training. The essence or concept of sport is to get away with the toils of life and have some fun. Master Funakoshi was against tournaments but I remember Nakayama Sensei telling him that it was a good way to promote the art and introduce it to the public. Nakayama Sensei stressed that it is not about trophies and medals but to bring the

art into the public eye. Master Jigoro Kano also recommended that Master Funakoshi have a ranking system as a motivational tool. These old masters were training for personal development and didn't need these kind of external rewards. But the times changed and people think and train for different reasons. The environment and the economic situations are all very different. But these masters reached a very high level with the old methods. That's why I keep training—to reach their level of excellence. That's the real challenge for the modern martial artists.

The most important thing is do your best. Not only in karate but in everything you do in your life. We are all human beings, there no way we can be perfect. But the idea of getting better and better everyday is what's important. ☻

Yoshiharu
Osaka

In 1966, I entered Takushoku University and trained there for more than four years. Eventually, I was asked to join the JKA instructor's course. The training was very hard. The atmosphere was very competitive and that made everything more difficult and tougher than any other place. I really enjoyed my time there because there was a sense of honor in winning trophies and tournaments for your university.

I was fortunate to have trained under one of the most knowledgeable instructors in the history of karate, Nakayama Sensei. He always emphasized the importance of the basics. We did a lot of kihon, regardless of our rank and position.

TECHNIQUE

Once you have been taught the correct body mechanics and physical elements of a technique, you'll see that those are relevant to how the human body moves and they have nothing to do with the color of your skin or your genetics. Correct technique is the result of a natural movement. If the technique is correctly practiced, the actions are harmonious, relaxed and powerful. The problem arises when people don't learn the right way and then go and teach incorrectly.

KATA

Kata should be kept as the original form that was developed. Kata represent the history of our art, and we can't change it as we please. The practitioner will put his own flavor [into it], but he shouldn't alter the form to suit himself. Perfection in kata is something impossible to attain, but it is the goal we all should try to reach. It is an impossible goal, but that's why it is a life experience. The real challenge is in every time we do the movement and in every single time we repeat the kata. There is no goal in kata training. The goal is the training itself.

In order to understand kata, it is important that the practitioners understand the process and evolution of that particular form. The old masters used kata as a way of passing their knowledge and personal experiences to future generations. This is the main reason why a kata may have many variations. Nakayama Sensei used kata as a training method for achieving technical perfection and bringing all the necessary attributes to the body of the practitioner. I personally believe that the old masters wanted us to participate in kata by using their knowledge as a sounding board for us to develop and research new and different possibilities that adapt to our time. We need to study and develop methods for applications based on our own bodies and levels of understanding. I believe that it is here when we can find a link between kata and the personal expression in kumite. Knowing all shotokan kata without having the proper understanding and feeling for each form is useless. Personal expression of the art must be emphasized here.

BUDO

In Budo, expression of an art can be interpreted as strength by some people, and at the same time, elegance by another. In essence, a genuine art such as karate will never be created until the artist is able to train his mind and body constantly and is able to acquire essential vigor to reach a stage of personal expression. In order to reach this stage, he must continually apply research and discipline. Karate techniques have not changed, but they have developed, which is different. The developments and modification of the techniques have been the product of a very intensive study. The only reason why these were done was to create a more efficient karate technique. They were not done for the idiosyncrasy of one particular individual. Unfortunately, I have seen basic karate techniques changed by some individual because of his inability to perform the technique correctly. JKA karate tries to make the body stronger and the techniques more powerful. It is based on physics and principles of body mechanics. Shotokan is a system that is based on the expansion of the body and using the natural power of it to perform the techniques. The movements are big most of the time, and this can be used later in time to improve health and other physical benefits, too.

SPORT

I don't think sport competition has to interfere in the development of true karate-do. Competition is a part of the training and can be helpful if it is properly used. It is a phase of the art that teaches things that we can't learn in

89

the dojo. It requires a different mental discipline and a different kind of self-control. This is the main reason why Nakayama Sensei began the competitions. But in karate-do we emphasize the complete process, the continued effort of becoming a better budoka. Competition has its place in karate, but its place is not in the regular basic training. Sometimes I get too worried because the emphasis these days is too much on tournaments and championships rather than in developing the important principles and ethics of karate as a way of life. The goal of Budo is to develop the practitioner as a warrior and as a human being. Some people think of a budoka as a warrior, and this is not correct in Budo, although it was correct in the old bujutsu because a practitioner needed to have extensive knowledge of fighting because he was facing enemies in the battlefield. Budo

involves more than fighting, and in fact, learning fighting arts is not the main goal in Budo practice. The idea of Budo, as Nayakama Sensei described it, is "to gain deep knowledge of the [our] chosen art to perfect our character and see clearly in our own nature and existence." And karate-do can help you to do that.

When you quit competition, the meaning of being strong reaches another level. You try to become strong and powerful to use your body properly for karate-do. You study your body and find out that going back to the basics is the secret. Karate technique will keep improving no matter what. And I hope future generations understand what they are doing so they can develop new technologies for training and [new] ways of using the body to perform karate better.

PHILOSOPHY

Karate has to be a reflection of who you are. And nobody is the same at 20 as he is at 50. Karate matures with age, and you karate must reflect your personal maturity as a human being. The natural body instinct slows down with age, but you have to keep training to revert this process back as much as you can. Train to develop focus and muscle control. These elements will be present during all of your years of karate, regardless of your age. Funakoshi Sensei always mentioned that karate should be used for perfection of character. The intelligent practitioner will change and adapt his training to his age. Karate is based on hard training and sacrifice, but there is also joy and fun. ◉

Osamu

Ozawa

My family was not rich but we were well off. I guess my parents had a lot of dreams for me—I would grow and mature, attend the University, and enter the family firm. But I guess that was a dream destined not to be. Life, pre-war, was very, very strict and very disciplined. It was a time of rising Japanese militancy in people minds. I remember that both judo and kendo were part of the educational system for imparting the ways of the warrior to the young. I wanted to be a professional military man but my mother was disgusted with the idea. I went to a junior military school and applied. I took the test but I failed. It was very demanding physically and mentally. Out of every 100 applicants, one was selected. My family was very disappointed with me. My mother was unhappy and my father didn't understand because he wanted me to attend the university to study business.

KARATE

I remember that nearly 80 people signed up for the university karate team. Mr. Ito gave a short lecture on the history and traditions of karate and then an explanation of the art. He made us try the

makiwara. I had trained before, and I had struck makiwara to toughen my hands. But many there had never seen the striking pole—then it was wound with tough rope. Mr. Ito commanded me to hit the makiwara 50 times with each hand. It didn't bother me but those who had never struck it were a different matter! Their hands were split and bleeding—some even cried.

"Today is your day to decide—stay or go," the seniors said. About 30 stayed. Over half indicated that they wanted to go. For those who stayed they announced that the training "was going to be different from then on; six days a week, six hours a day." The training became more severe than military discipline. In the military, superiors could beat subordinates with a bo, or order troop punishment but in karate we would be left sitting in *seiza* for hours, forbidden to move. Being struck in the face was common punishment. The training was hard, terrible hard. It was about spiritual training...but technically...I don't know now. I have to confess that I was frightened: I didn't want to stay, but I was scared to quit because there was a formal ritual to say goodbye to all the members training in the dojo. It was a very formal occasion. The members were lined up according to seniority, from junior to senior. Then you approached them one by one. You said, "Goodbye," then the person would strike you in the face. I was really scared to quit!

GICHIN FUNAKOSHI

Funakoshi Sensei was a very strong, very wise man. I don't think a day goes by that I do not think of him. I meditate in my dojo sitting before his photograph in the *kamiza*, and burn incense in his memory. Before the war, I don't really think we believed he was a great man. Sensei was very soft spoken; he would observe as seniors Obata, Hironishi and Tagaki supervised the training. Master Funakoshi would walk up and down the lines and stop and talk with every student and correct this or that. Sometimes at night I go to the dojo and practice my kata singing a poem written by Sensei Funakoshi that begins; "There is an island to the south, where there is a beautiful art. This is karate."

WORLD WAR II

The war was a big change for many of us. A lot of classmates were being called up for military service and faces began to disappear from the dojo. Whenever anyone left, we had a farewell party. We would gather in a restaurant and wish farewell to our comrade. We would toast their fortunes. There wasn't time to hold a farewell party for me. I was called up to serve in the Japanese Imperial Navy Air Fleet!

The war times I think it is something that is best left in the past. I cannot describe well what we felt. It was a time of purity—great emotional strength. We believed in our minds, in our hearts and souls, that we were to lay down our lives for the nation. It was very beautiful—but very hard to explain. I had a flight accident that punctured one lung. I spent six months in two different hospitals recovering. Physical injuries

heal but the devastation done to Japan looked as if it could never be healed. Japan was a sea of rubble. In Tokyo, most of the people had no housing, not even huts or tents. Everything lay in ruin. My karate colleagues, the practitioners of the first great age of Japanese karate, had been scattered to the wind.

Sensei Funakoshi had gone to Kyushu in 1945, after the fall of Okinawa. He discovered that his wife was ill and dying. These were days of dark discovery. He did not return to Tokyo until about 1947. He looked very old when he returned from Kyushu. He had lost his wife, and many fine, wonderful karate students. I remember one, a much senior practitioner from Takushoku University. He had been the captain of the team and he was a very great student of Sensei's. We used to fear him because he was really powerful. In those days there was no tournament but after exchanging training, we would free spar. Sensei Funakoshi was very sad when he heard of this death.

After the war, Funakoshi Sensei looked old but he remained healthy. Whenever we needed him, we went to pick him up. It was interesting because even if he looked old, when he changed into his uniform he was full of energy! Of course, he was not as active as before the war, but it was a truly honor to have him two or three times a month. There is no value that can be placed on having known him.

JKA

It was around 1949 when seniors Obata, Tagaki, Nakayama, Fukui and Ito got together. They decided on inviting Sensei to be Instructor Emeritus. Senior Nakayama was given the duty of being the active Chief Instructor; the others assisting. A tiny office was set up in Ginza. The original dojo—the Shotokan—had been bombed during the war. There was no place to train and some wanted to rebuild the old Shotokan building. This is how the Japan Karate Association (JKA) was created. Later on, in 1949, we decided to create a national organization and Sensei Hidetaka Nishiyama was assigned the responsibilities of technical advisor.

The reunification of Shotokan Karate was completed in 1952, but Master Funakoshi never wanted his karate to be called "Shotokan"— the Hall of Shoto. He always called his art "Japanese Karate," because it was of and for Japan. That is why there was a JKA and not a group called "Shotokan."

UNIFICATION

There were some differences in the karate styles but not between the masters such as Yamaguchi, Funakoshi, Mabuni, et cetera. All those differences lay between the young students, and not the masters. I remember we managed to give a dinner for all the masters. Unfortunately, the unification of all karate styles was a dream that for whatever reasons, and there were many, failed to come about. ◉

Masahiko

Tanaka

My family was constantly moving, and I didn't have any opportunity to make friends and stay with them for a long period of time. I would pack my knapsack and go hiking into the mountains alone. I believe this influenced me greatly. I chose rugby at my school because it seemed like it was the toughest activity, and I wanted to prove that I was a man. In fact, I can say that all my karate power comes from those sprints during my rugby years because everything was ankles, knees and hips. Rugby helped to mold my legs in those early years.

I went to Nihon University. I studied economics in the footsteps of my father who died when I was 19. A friend of mine at the university took me to a karate dojo. Yaguchi Sensei was the teacher there. I joined, but I never told my mother that I did. I didn't want her to worry about me learning how to fight. Later on, someone saw me fight and invited me to participate in the Kanto Area Championship. My team took first place.

Already then, karate was my life. I was a *san-dan* at the time, and I really wanted to take the courses for *kenshusei* [student instructor]

at the JKA Headquarters. They refused my request because there weren't enough funds to support a student instructor at the time. However, if I could support myself, they said that I would be allowed to enter the course. I started to look for any kind of job that would allow me to pay my bills, and it didn't matter to me what kind of work it was. I was everything from a river man to a real estate agent. For a year I transported logs along canals. When doing this, you have to actually ride the logs, so I thought of it as a training for my legs. Gradually, as my balance improved, I fell into the water less and less.

SPORT

I was sent to Denmark in 1975 but I kept training so I could compete in the World Karate Championships that were held that year in Los Angeles, California. I used some of the Danish karateka to prepare myself for that tournament, and I found out later on that they weren't enjoying the training with me at all. It turns out that they thought I was very hard with them and with myself, but that was the only way I knew how to get better ... training as hard as I can. I ended up winning the world title. In the final, I had to face Oishi Takeshi Sensei, and he was one of the best in the world. He was the kumite champion the previous four years.

I came out of retirement in 1986 to enter the 29th JKA Championship and it was a good challenge for me. I was 45 years old, and I knew I presented a challenge to all the young fighters. I was defeated in the quarterfinals and felt a little disappointed, but I wanted to prove myself that I could contest the young champions in competition ... not just in the dojo. I did this for my own satisfaction. I love to fight and that urge was with me for some time.

PHILOSOPHY

Karate was created and developed as a self-defense method. Funakoshi Sensei saw the flaws in trying to keep a warrior mentality in times of peace and developed a new approach to the art. Fighting has always been and always will be an important part of karate because that is where the true spirit of Budo is absorbed. Therefore, karate-do is an art because it allows us to reach higher levels of existence as human beings. It is also an art because the students need to learn the principles, work hard and develop their own way of expressing karate through their bodies. Art is not something that you develop by simply copying others. I can copy a Picasso's painting, but it doesn't make me an artist. To be an artist, and every karate-ka should be one, we need to learn how to express—in our own words—what we have learnt from our teacher. If the art is to survive, this is the only way.

Karate is an art, and art is—more than anything—an expression. When you see a kata performed well, you realize that immediately. As artists, we all strive for perfection. In our case, we should strive for perfection in technique, even though we will never achieve it.

Karate is a martial art and a way of life, not only a physical activity that has a sportive side to it. Master Funakoshi said karate should

be used as a tool to develop and perfect one's character ... both physically and mentally. When we talk about karate as a way of life, we open the possibility of many interpretations. It is interesting that, regardless of how people understand it, there are some fundamental truths to it that don't change. Through many years of intense training under our teachers, we learn the basics of both the technical and spiritual side of the

art. We follow our sensei, and by watching and listening to him, we reach a high level of skill and understanding. So, in some sort of way, we are following the way of life that has been handed down through the years. Now it is up to us to find our own way or put it together in a personal format that applies to our life. The quest is now to make it our own. It is important to respect and give credit to the teachers, because without them, our spiritual growth probably would never come about. And without their guidance in training, we wouldn't be who we are today.

JKA KARATE

In the JKA, we worked hard to develop a form of karate that uses the human body in the best possible way when it comes to utilizing all muscles and joints in the body to generate power. It is a very simple concept, but it is a difficult task to achieve. It's a straight down-the-line karate that places emphasis on good form, speed and kime. Is not that what any karate should be? JKA Shotokan is more a method or approach to karate than a separate style. Unfortunately, many people don't understand this. Every single punch and every single block and kick must be fast, powerful and precise, and they should have kime and power. These are the tools the artist must use. Considering this, it is not difficult to incorporate softer approaches to use the "tools" because the elements are already there. You may add a

circular motion to the way your body moves, but when you punch, block or kick … you do it with power and determination. You must learn not only how to make karate natural to you but also how to strengthen your body without stressing it more than necessary. Wrong technique brings a lot of injuries.

Karate is not just a sport

or a physical activity; it is a martial art and a way of life. A way of life is always part of us in every minute of our existence.

Unfortunately, many people want to make money with karate, even if they are not fully qualified to do it. For me it is more rewarding to study the art, follow your teacher and try to be the best human being you can. This is traditional Budo, and this is what I believe. If karate training teaches us anything, it teaches us that the truth is always harder to take and less attractive than we would like. I think that true traditional karate will [eventually] be lost if there aren't any instructors or students who adhere to the traditional methods and values of karate and Budo.

Karate must be followed the way it is, and you cannot try to change it. When you get into your car to go to work, you follow the street, right? You don't create new streets or simply go ahead because you don't like curves. You follow the streets. That's the way karate is and the way it should be practiced.

Funakoshi Sensei clearly explained that the goal of karate is perfection of character. Therefore, we have to look at it as a lifetime training and philosophy that involves the body, the mind and also the spirit. In life, the goals that are worth keeping are the ones that take time and effort to achieve. Those things are not achieved quickly and require sincere dedication and good character.

Karate training is a mirror of life, and the way you live your life must go hand in hand with the way your train. ◉

Mikio
Yahara

Shotokan was the original style. What I teach is that karate is changing, and it is possible that it could disappear. I know karate as a martial art, but now it seems more like dancing. I would like to return to the original karate … to its sources. Budo karate, as far as I am concerned, is a situation in which I may finish my opponent definitively by one killing blow. My work basically consists in forming ways and methods to increase my technical level to the perfection I require and that is one blow should be enough to cause an opponent's defeat.

True Budo karate has very effective techniques and I want to teach my students that they are capable of winning any competition. I want people to know and learn my techniques and understand my aim for perfection. Sports karate is very popular now and many people consider karate a game. These people usually forget about karate immediately after competition. If necessary, I would like my students to be able to use karate in real life, but I don't want them to treat it like it was strictly a game.

Karate has no philosophy. Some people think that the tradition of karate came from Buddhism and karate has a connection with the

absolute, space and universe, but I don't believe in that. My philosophy is to knock my opponent out with one technique. One finishing blow!

In the beginning, it is good for a student to concentrate on a few things that he can develop strongly. I don't like to give students too many things to concentrate on. Not aikido one day, the next karate, judo and then something else! That is not good. Unfortunately, some students think this is the correct way because they want too much too soon, and there is nothing the instructor can do about it. Their minds are diffused over too many ideas. That's why it is very important to train the mind of the student in the right direction. If the student has "no mind" in training, he will get into these kinds of situations and will make incorrect decisions. Hard, physical training helps to develop the right mind for karate. And technique isn't the only important thing; you must also make good, true karate.

The makiwara is not only a tool to be used for conditioning, but when used correctly, it makes the body strong, especially the hips and hara areas. Makiwara training brings control to the technique. Traditional karate training places great emphasis upon the mind, and makiwara training helps this, because in many ways, it is the basis of the art.

I am against the type of competition that promotes the development of game karate. I frequently have debates and conversations with representatives of other organizations to defend my opinion about karate, and it is possible that my actions remind them of true karate.

Many people don't understand my karate. You have to be spiritually strong because karate must be spiritually strong, too. Then the correct technique will grow from it. I have seen some people who think they are strong, but the truth is they are bigheaded. I look for perfection in what I do, but I still have a long road ahead. Technique comes to some students quickly and to others slowly. But if they keep training hard and follow the principle of *nichi nichi no keko* (train harder over and over again), they will be alright.

The way we always competed was very Budo-oriented. We always looked for the "kill." Since the advent and growth of freestyle karate, the main goal in many dojo around the world is simply competition. Unfortunately, many associations that regulate the competition rules allow participants to do strange things. For instance, punching with good and strong positioning and scoring with a simple touch is one of those. Also, contestants lack zanchin. They concentrate more on what the referee will say than on their opponent. They should look at the opponent and not the referee. Forget the referee! Many students around the world never learn this serious approach to kumite karate, and the art becomes a simple sport. This approach brings a lack of

confidence to the students simply due to the fact that they haven't been trained properly. They must be trained to kill with one blow, but they also have to learn how to control their power and techniques.

Is it possible to be happy after suffering a defeat? When a strong person loses, he doesn't feel any satisfaction, and he will never find both spiritual and psychological victory. However, victory and spiritual satisfaction could come later, because your defeat stimulates new feats. You try to improve your skill, and as a result, you win. In this case, you will understand that the victory is the result of your last defeat.

Recently, many people have turned to Zen, and there are many books about this; however, it is a fake. Why? Of course, Zen could be indicated in a fight. But what is the sense of Zen? If two opponents had a knife, it would be too easy if they just killed each other. In this case, it would be an ordinary murder. Both of the opponents would die, and they would be absolutely tranquil, because there is no difference for each opponent. But there is a significant problem. Each adversary keeps wondering what will occur in case of a mistake? Maybe someone will be wounded. The body becomes enslaved and the mind just thinks about fear. This fear disturbs the use of your actual power. Kumite teaches us to stay tranquil. If you follow the Zen way, you will have the emptiness in your mind while doing kumite. Fear and thought disappear from your mind, and you don't feel the fear. In this moment, you are able to demonstrate your true power ... the power that is available only to you. No emotions, no thoughts about past and future. This is Zen. That is why people who write books about Zen Buddhism in the martial arts without experi-

encing serious fighting or mortal combat are liars.

I like to read very much. Usually, I read books about the samurai and how they bravely passed away as a result of hara-kiri (ritual suicide). It is very important for me, and I will tell you about this without any embellishment. Three of my friends have died in such a way and the last one occurred in December 2003. The most courageous way to die from hara-kiri is the crisscross. [Using a sword], you go from left to right and then bottom to top. This gives you the hieroglyph "ju," and that means 10. Maybe you know the famous Japanese writer Yukio Mishima; perhaps you even read his books. He was my student. We trained together for one and half a years. He was much older than me. When he was 45, I was

24. One week before his passing we were training together. After training, we were in the traditional Japanese bath or *furo*. His behavior was normal, he laughed and nobody—even I—suspected that he was going to leave this life. Something like this is a very important decision, and I am sure that one week prior to his death he certainly knew that he would do it. I very much respect him for it, and he was a really great person.

Everybody should ask himself the following question: "What is the most important thing for me in karate?" I think that we all should practice karate with the same spirit, mood and ideas. Likely, people who practice karate with very similar ideas have identical inquiries, needs and purposes. The most important thing that I want to pass on to you all is that you should never forget about the source of karate, its basic functions and purposes. If you ignore this and do not diligently execute all techniques, you will absolutely walk the other way, which is very far from the karate that I try to teach. Control your ego properly because the true enemy is inside yourself, and this is the toughest opponent to beat.

Koss

Yokota

I started my martial arts in 1960 with judo. I was 13 years old. My father was a black belt in Kodokan judo. When I asked him which martial art I should learn, he encouraged me to take up judo. There was no judo club at the junior high school I was attending, so I went to the district police station where they had judo and kendo training. This was mainly for the policemen, but it was open to the public. I went for three years and got a black belt. A new student— who was a little different from most—joined the class towards the end of the period. As soon as he was thrown down, he jumped up like a bouncing ball and took a different stance that was much wider than a normal judo stance. I asked him why he was doing this, and he said that he was getting into a karate stance. Even though I knew about karate, I had very little knowledge about it, so I asked him about it after the training. He told me that he was a karate practitioner and was taking judo to better his fighting skill. At that time, I believed that judo was the deadliest art, so I asked if he agreed. To my surprise, he said karate was much deadlier in a hand-to-hand combat. He showed me how he could attack me and knock me down while I was trying to grab his hand or *gi*. If I could grab him, I had a chance to throw him down, but his fast punch and kick would surely get me first. So, this opened my eyes, and I switched to karate in 1963. Again, my high school did not have a karate club, so I joined the YMCA Karate Club in my hometown, which was Kobe. The club, although I didn't know it, was a JKA organization.

When I started karate training. I wanted to get as much training as possible. My first sensei was Master Sugano, 9th dan JKA in Kobe, Japan. I trained under him between 1963 and 1966, as well as from 1981 to 1983. Unfortunately, he passed away at the age of 72.

Karate was little known in the 1960s and early 1970s. Judo and jiu-jitsu were more popular, so I initially taught both judo and karate. When the students saw the karate techniques—particularly the kicks—I got instant respect. Many of them were familiar with boxing, but kicking was unknown and maybe a little bit mysterious. They were impressed not only by the kicking techniques but also by the sophisticated body movements like rotation, jumping, squatting and lying down ... movements that are uniquely found in karate.

My belief is that a karate instructor, at least a certified one, must be able to perform better than any of his students who may be younger or physically bigger and stronger.

I tell my students all the time that thinking is most important in karate training. It is very easy and becomes comfortable for a student to get in automatic pilot mode. A student tends to follow an instructor's commands blindly without thinking about the technique he is performing. Improvements will not occur only with repetitions. Each student has different challenges and must make appropriate efforts during the movements to improve himself. To be able to make such an effort, a student needs to know what and how to correct the flaws and mistakes. In Japan, an instructor rarely makes any comments. In the 1960s, we had to learn only from watching the senior students, senpai or sensei. I used to picture my sensei's

movements and attempt to copy them. The system and expectations were that only the talented and lucky ones would advance. Non-Japanese instructors often take time and effort to explain and comment on the technique and this can be helpful.

Karate is changing, even in Japan as the tournament karate is becoming more popular. Thus, the introduction of a sports mentality is unavoidable. The Budo aspect was emphasized more and the rules and dojo etiquette were followed much more strictly in the past. Budo means a way of life and a sickness is a part of your life. Thus, we train with fever and headache. The formality, unfortunately, is disappearing as well. In many dojo, line-up rituals in *seiza* and bowing are no longer exercised. Bowing etiquette between the students and to the sensei are enforced and followed less. Such etiquette is a crucial part of Budo, so it is my opinion that we must never forget or ignore it.

KATA

If you do a kata without thinking, that kata will be not too far off from a dance. If a movement or an application does not make sense in a kata, the student must challenge the movement and investigate it until it does. If an application does not work or looks unrealistic, he needs to find out why. It is a waste of time to do a kata in which the movements lack the meaning of fighting or some other reasonable meaning. This approach is needed more in kumite. It is more difficult here as one needs to think in a hurry during kumite. The student has more time in kata, as your imaginary opponent is much more patient and generous in giving you time to think. In kumite, most of the time, you do not dictate the time. You need to think of the distance, timing and target, in addition to the stances and the very technique to apply.

Different ryu are important when you practice karate as martial arts. There cannot be one ryu that transcends all styles, as our bodies and minds are all different. Can we say European fencing is better than Japanese kendo or Chinese sword fighting? Certainly not. Each karate ryu has the basic concepts of fighting style and methodology. Some emphasize close fighting like goju-ryu and others long-distance fighting like shotokan. Then the techniques such as stances must change according to the varied distance from the opponent. Different masters had different ideas and skilled technique, but no one master was perfect. There is always something you can learn from another style. The quality varies because the skill level and experience of instructors vary. You may find an excellent shotokan dojo with an excellent instructor, but you may also find a bad one in the same city if the instructor is not certified or has little teaching experience. The same can be said of any style. The strength and weaknesses of a style should not be judged by the performance of one dojo or even by a group of dojo. If you wish to compare or examine the technique and methodology of a certain ryu, you need to go to the source, which means you go to the headquarters or the original master.

We should keep the traditional styles or ryu independent and practiced separately. Personally, I am against the idea of mixing them up. However, karate is a fluid art and each style does change as it is handed down through the generations. In the process, there may be an exceptionally talented master who may be capable of incorporating two or more styles and estab-

lish his own style. That is possible but nevertheless unlikely.

There are different kinds of karate. It can be a sport (tournament), martial arts, self-defense or an exercise to improve health. They are all fine, and it is up to the practitioners to choose which karate they wish to practice. When I was younger, I enjoyed tournaments, but I graduated from them 20 years ago. Now, I train for martial arts (Budo) and health purposes. I teach martial arts karate at my dojo but, if some of the students want to participate in tournaments, I do not object to it. Even though we do not practice anything in particular to prepare for a tournament, I encourage the young students to get some experience and enjoy the excitement. The unfortunate thing is that many of the tournament competitors believe there is not much difference between sport karate and Budo karate. I feel this is my job to teach my students how Budo training is different from tournament karate training. The philosophical basis for my training is Budo, a way of life. This is a way for me to grow and improve as a karate-ka and simply as a human being.

Karate will change and that is a natural process. It is our responsibility to keep karate at its best and improve it so we can hand down the arts to the next generation.

I personally oppose adding karate to the Olympics. I am sure the Olympics will make karate even more popular, and this can be a welcome effect to many instructors. However, I am afraid the downside outweighs the benefits.

It is necessary for the instructors to encourage the students to try

to win competitions and go for the next rank, but I believe it is much more important to teach them that karate-do practice means a lifetime endeavor and rank advancement is only a part of karate and not the ultimate goal. It is also ultimately the instructor's responsibility to improve himself continuously so that he can provide the exciting training to the advanced students for many years.

Master Nakayama was great because he built a JKA empire, which then the world's largest traditional karate organization. It was not only the largest but also the most solid karate organization in the 1970s and 1980s. He established a *kenshu-sei* system and dispatched many talented instructors to the world in the 1950s and 1960s to propagate karate. I believe this is the main reason why shotokan became the brand name among the traditional karate styles around the world. JKA was also most respected as the best fighting style in

Japan for many years. It is a shame that Master Nakayama passed away so young. He was really the axis that gave the tight cohesion among the JKA instructors, not only in Japan but also around the world. He was a true gentleman and a karate master. I sincerely miss his leadership and teaching.

117

"The perfect state of existence lies between what is substantial and what is insubstantial."
—Masatoshi Nakayama